POSTULATE
Like A PRO

How To Use The Spiritual Universe
To Get What You Want

10-10-10
Publishing

TABLE OF CONTENTS

SECTION 2

More *Postulate Like A Pro* Stories

WHAT IS A POSTULATE?

Informally, a postulate is a thought you have that actually comes true in the Physical Universe.

Let me explain. When someone splashes you, you then notice that your bathing suit is wet. The cause is the splashing and the effect is the wetness of your bathing suit. No surprise. The cause is in the Physical Universe so you can easily see it. When you see both the cause and the effect, there is no mystery. No miracle. But, when the cause is in the Spiritual Universe (and hence in some sense hidden from plain view) and the effect is plainly evident in the Physical Universe, there is mystery. "Where did that come from? How did that happen? It must be a miracle."

You might casually mention to your friend, "Remember Ralph from High School?" Then, the phone rings and it's Ralph!!! Was it a coincidence? If it was simply a coincidence, then the world is random—that's not a pleasant thought. If it was caused, who caused it? The answer is that you caused it by thinking of Ralph. Your thoughts are in the Spiritual Universe. The Spiritual Universe causes the whole Physical Universe, not just Ralph phoning.

Your postulates cause your entire Physical Universe. You have a Physical Universe and it is different from mine. I have a sweet caring wife, a loving marriage, a gorgeous log cabin out in the wilderness, a healthy body, a powerful mind, ten devoted staff, two wonderful daughters, a cuddly cat named Friendly, very high income and very high net worth. How did all this happen? Is it all just a coincidence? Every single aspect of my Physical Universe is a consequence of the thoughts (which are in the Spiritual Universe) coming true.

Sometimes the thoughts are conscious like you may think intently about getting the woman/man of your dreams, a million-dollar net worth, health, etc. Sometimes, the thoughts are very, very quiet messages that are so subtle they are easy to dismiss. "Turn down 8th Street instead of 4th Street today." Or, "Gee, I've never gone into that store, I think I'll just go into it today."

Let me relate a very subtle message I received recently …

> I was returning from a run along Lakeshore Road recently. Passing a Starbucks, I decided to buy a treat for my wife Karyn. I jogged home balancing the Cappuccino. When I got to the Lakeshore entrance of my high-rise luxury condo tower, I was eager to enter that south door to go up the south side elevator to my condo suite on the south side of the tower. I was particularly eager to get to my wife as soon as possible so that the coffee could be as hot as possible.
>
> I heard a quiet subtle voice "Use the north entrance." I dismissed that as silly and wrong. If I walked all the way over to the north entrance, I would simply have to walk all the way back to the south side of the tower to get to my wife in our south-side suite. It made no sense. Further, any delay just makes the coffee colder.
>
> I did go to the north door, all the way chastising myself for being so foolish.

Just as I approached the north door, my wife drove out of the underground parking garage, right beside the north door, saw me, saw the coffee, rolled down her driver's window and took the coffee from my outstretched hand as she drove by, without pausing. Perfectly choreographed.

Split-second timing.

That experience is now a sacred incident in our marriage.

If I had done the 'right' thing of using the 'correct' south door, I would have entered our suite and found it empty. Then, when my wife returned from her chores several hours later, I would have handed her totally cold coffee and it would have been a huge fail instead of a dazzling postulate.

That's a postulate.

You've heard the quote: "Thoughts are things." But it is not true. Why? Because thoughts are in the Spiritual Universe and things are in the Physical Universe. However, there is a correct quote: "Thoughts create things." Yes, that's the truth.

To learn more about the Spiritual Universe, contact help@aaron.com and ask for information about a powerful 3-day spiritual workshop with the very unusual name of Mulberry Hill Gang.

SECTION 1

ORBIT™ COACH
AND
ORBIT™ COACHING CLIENTS

THE WOMAN OF MY DREAMS AND A MILLION DOLLARS

Raymond Aaron
ORBIT™ Coach

I teach a rather unique spiritual workshop with the most unusual name, The Mulberry Hill Gang™ (MHG). The promise is that you get whatever you wish. It's a giant promise and I truly deliver on that promise.

I had been alone and lonely for a decade. I wanted a woman in my life, but found no one. My friend Wendy recommended I teach my amazing MHG once again and instead of being just the teacher, I should be the teacher and a student. She further explained that if I were also a student, I could postulate the woman of my dreams just showing up. I was so excited that I added a second postulate that I would earn $1 million faster than anyone on earth had ever earned a million dollars.

My step-daughters imposed a rule on me that I could not date anyone younger than them. That seems reasonable.

My business partner Geoff, an accountant, imposed yet another rule on me: that I could not date revenue or expenses. What? What does that even mean? He explained that revenue was clients and expenses meant staff. I accepted.

The first day of my miracle workshop MHG arrived … and there she was in the front row. Young. Beautiful. Sexy. Stunningly-dressed. Brilliant answers to my questions. She laughed at my jokes. She asked insightful questions. I was smitten.

But I needed to know her age because of my commitment to my stepdaughters. I asked every participant to submit their birthday with year. I discarded all others and looked only at hers. She was just months older than my older stepdaughter. Phew.

But what was worse is that she was for sure a client. I checked our company database and she wasn't in it. But she was definitely in a paid course. So, I strolled up to her at a break to ask why she wasn't in our database. She said she had not paid for the course, rather her boss had paid for it and was called away to China on short notice to inspect a factory. He had forgotten what the course was about but gave her the ticket to attend. So, impossibly, she was attending a paid course … but she hadn't paid. Hence, she was not a client. And, she was old enough.

On our first date, it got even weirder. I look much younger than my actual age, so I confessed to her my age. I could see she was subtracting her age from my age and she said 17. She made an unhappy look on her face meaning that that was the very very outside limit of what she could accept. However, she made a subtraction error. I'm 27 years older. But, I wanted to be her lover, not her math tutor, so I said nothing. Fortunately, she fell in love with me before she discovered her subtraction error.

And that's how the Spiritual Universe removed all obstacles to allow me to find the woman of my dreams on the very first day of MHG.

And, as an enticing footnote, you will recall that I added that I wanted to earn one million dollars faster than anyone on earth had ever earned that amount of money. Shortly after that offering of MHG, a promoter called me to ask if I would like to present at a giant summit to be attended by 17,000 eager entrepreneurs. The promoter gave me the very best speaker slot, every seat was filled, and I earned over one million dollars in that speech. That was by far the most I'd ever earned and since that date I have never earned anywhere near that amount since. Just once. Just from that startling postulate!

Please connect with Raymond Aaron at help@aaron.com to be considered to attend the powerful spiritual workshop: Mulberry Hill Gang.

LOVE THY NEIGHBOR
AS THY SELF

David Currie
ORBIT™ Coaching Client

In April 2020, less than a year ago as I write this, I was driving home from an early morning breakfast with my friend George, who had noticeably lost weight since I had seen last seen him 6 months earlier. As I traveled home, the voice in my head intoned "No more excuses!". I had been losing weight and gradually improving my health, but it was time to get serious about my diet, my body, and my mind.

A few months earlier I put myself on medical leave at a company I co-owned. I could no longer make it up the flight of steps to our offices without two long pauses to catch my breath and recover from dizziness. These health issues had been gradually getting worse. I continued working part-time from home until my retirement in early 2021

Today, I am 50 pounds lighter, a teetotaler, meditating and exercising daily, off half a dozen medications and as fit as I have been since my teens. I am inspired and excited to co-author a book called For the Good of All, NOW! Create Your Own Circle of Happiness and Serenity—From Local to Global. The publication of this book will mark the launch of a global movement serving as a path for humanity to achieve the evolutionary breakthrough to Oneness that will ultimately save the human race. This is not a foregone conclusion given the entrenched forces aligned to thwart this paradigm shift. And it is definitely leagues away from the life I imagined for myself as a child.

There were a few inklings of the future David in those tender years. I was drawn to the underdog and fiercely opposed to injustice. On my bedroom wall, I hung two oversized posters: at the top of the bed a huge picture of Martin Luther King Jr. facing him at the other end of the bed, an equally large poster, the famous picture of blue planet Earth floating in dark space. These choices were in a physical world sense quite common. Planet earth captured on film was transformational on a human level. Martin Luther King Jr. was a prophet who became a martyr to our better selves, and in the mold of Mahatma Gandhi inspired millions of people, as they both continue to do even to this day.

Fifty years ago, in 1971, I experienced an event that would shape my life, for better and for worse, from that day forward.

It was a beautiful summer's day in my 18th year, I was driving an old, small, tank-like truck. Suddenly, I was forced to swerve out of the lane I was traveling in. I smacked head-on into a much smaller car coming from the opposite direction. To this day, I can and do replay the scene in my mind's eye as crisply as if I were there when I came to—in full vivid technicolor. My truck was on top of the hood of smaller car. The engine racing. Someone yelled to turn it off. There were three occupants, all just a few years older than I was. None of them were stirring. The police took me to the station instead of a hospital. I drifted in and out of consciousness, but they never answered my burning question about the people in the car. I was sure that the girl riding in the front passenger seat was dead. I finally got the truth from my friends (Jérôme, Betsy and Penny), who came to fetch me, that the young woman had died. I wished I were dead.

Twenty-four years later, during the night of September 6th and early morning of the 7th 1995, while Cal Ripken Jr. was breaking the consecutive-games-played record of Lou Gehrig the "Iron Horse", to assume his title as the "Iron Man" in Major League Baseball, I was having a heart attack. In the living room, holding my left arm, watching Mr. Ripken's feat, I swayed from one foot to the other to assuage the pain. A heart attack at 42! Somewhere deep inside me, was a recurring voice saying stop! That night it got really loud. Stop, the self-destruction and the indifference to your physical, mental, and emotional brokenness.

As I lay recovering in a hospital ICU bed, I promised to myself and to my wife that I would make some serious changes. Instead of the business rat race, I would embark on a "community building" career empowered by the notion of "giving back". I launched into it with gusto. I started a Heart Support Group with support from the local hospital. I became President of the local business association. It was in this capacity that I met recent arrivals to our area, Dot and Rae, who ran a small retreat center in the hills outside the village where my wife and I lived. Rae had discerned a pattern to my recurring heart issues since the '95 heart attack— angina, 3 stents and few scares. I found this to be a curious and interesting concept. Today, I know my spirit was whispering to me. My intention to be healthier had connected me to the right people, at the right time, in the right place.

I willingly underwent a deep introspective process with my new spirit guides. It didn't take long to identify the 1970's as the decade "of interest". BAM! Spirit figuratively had to clobber me in the head with a board. I suppose it is part of the craziness of my inner turmoil that I had never connected the heart attack to The Accident. How strange, looking back, at how blind I was to this connection. How grateful I was, and I continue to be, for my spirit guides intervention. One of the erroneous conclusions, as it turns out, was that The Accident broke my heart. Truthfully, my behavior and the stress of PTSD broke my heart. It took 50 years for me to find peace.

The second part, the Transformational Part of the therapy, involved a deep introspective exercise to uncover and express my life's guiding themes in three words. My answers were: Peace, Serenity, and Changing the World. Unlike Peace and Serenity, which have comprehensible definitions, "Changing the World" could mean pretty much anything. It might mean the world writ small as in "my world", or large as in the "big wide world", and anything in between. I have puzzled the meaning for the last 40 years.

During this period, I reached out to my older brother and he sent me a copy of M Scott Peck's "*The Different Drum-Community and Making Peace*". This work proved to be life-changing for me. He connected *Community* in the title to my new commitment to "building community".

I joined Dr. Peck's Foundation for Community Encouragement and reserved a space at a group-gathering in Western Massachusetts. By the time I arrived at the retreat center, I was in full 24-hour flu-symptom mode. Two guides at the reception desk, ML Healey and Jessica Zane, took me under their wings and settled me down in a private room. I had recovered sufficiently the next day to attend, albeit in a weakened state and for the following two days, I experienced, for the first time, the power of deep community. (I get goosebumps as I am writing this.)

At the end of the last day, as we were winding down, I was overcome by the ineffable sense that if someone were to come into our Circle and ask us to solve a world-sized challenge, we could easily devise the right solution. I had never felt such power. I had never felt such calmness. I had never felt such immersive love.

At the parting, ML and Jessica suggested that I ought to consider attending an upcoming workshop given by Joanna Macy who would become one of my most important teachers.

It is said that "when the pupil is ready, the teacher arises". I think often of the many teachers "arising" in my life: the 3 occupants of the car and especially the woman who died, my hero Martin Luther King, the picture that changed humanity and our relationship to planet Earth, my beloved parents and brother, Dot and Rae.

The teachers don't just appear. They appear as a result of being summoned. Sometimes by my intention, sometimes by the intentions of others. The point is that the appearance of the teacher is not happenstance. There is always meaning and purpose in her appearance.

Obviously, I have had the choice to heed or ignore these calls. I have heeded and ignored these "callings", to my detriment and ultimately my great benefit. My clear intention for you, is to suggest that you learn to recognize the callings and heed them.

In total, I have attended three Joanna Macy retreats and spent some very special moments beyond these special settings. Joanna's teachings and purpose are focused on Despair and Empowerment—powerful lessons for the chaos that is occurring now in this time of The Great Turning—as she has named it. Power lessons for me to learn and feel.

At the end of the first retreat, a woman whose name I never knew, presented me with two papers written in the first years of the current century by Terry Mollner. It was altogether a strange and memorable encounter.

Be aware of the "strange and memorable"! The moments you say to yourself: "that was weird". These moments stick to you. They are moments of great importance.

At the very end of the second retreat, at my request, Joanna, another fellow, and I led the group in a discussion regarding how to launch the Nuclear Guardianship Foundation. Joanna's work with survivors in the vicinity of the Chernobyl nuclear disaster seared this notion in her psyche. And she conceived the principles of Nuclear Guardianship to protect future generations from poisonous waste. Although, I was unsuccessful in translating my enthusiasm and the shared wisdom that came out of the discussion that night, the spirit of Guardianship, is an important part of the movement I describe in an upcoming book: *For the Good of All, NOW!*

Again, I have goosebumps as I am writing about the experience of the awesome sense of power unleashed that dark winter's evening. This time it felt to me like the floor itself and all assembled on it were pulsating and levitating. The whole room was completely engaged, energized with all minds, all hearts acting in unison contributing their shared practical wisdom to this vision so important to Joanna and me.

I imagine that chroniclers of miracles have had the same challenge in conveying the special unforgettable majesty of these moments. Words are insufficient to describe these experiences. They are rare, but like the less intensive callings, they too should be heeded.

In September 2001, Dot Maver returned from her work in Australia where she intended to recreate a "Share the Spirit of Peace" campaign here in the United States. I traveled from outside New York City to attend the first event in Vermont and volunteered to be the coordinator for the transportation of 40 young people from dozens of countries to attend the International Day of Peace at the UN and participate in a retreat. I ended up quitting my job to devote myself to this project, the tug was that strong. Not a popular decision in our household! But the inner voice was too strong.

In 2007, my wife and I moved back to Upstate New York to the area where she grew up and we met. It was love at first sight for me and within a year we were married—that was almost 42 years ago as I write this. I became involved in formalizing a nonprofit organization dedicated to promoting sustainability in the rust belt communities along the border with Pennsylvania. Our youngest board member, Hadassah, whose friendship I value so greatly, introduced me to David Sloan Wilson, a Distinguished Professor of Evolutionary Biology at SUNY Binghamton and the pre-eminent evolutionary biologist of our time. An inscription he dedicated in my copy of one of his books reads "To David, Soul Mate". Be awake to the presence of Soul Mates! (Aha, goosebumps again.)

Soon we were co-facilitating a reading group on the *Small Mart Revolution* by Michael Shuman, which led to a regular community "Cabaret" series, a casual group of inquiry, with far ranging topics related to our community. We soon realized that we both shared great excitement about the work of Elinor Ostrum who, despite winning a Nobel Prize in Economics was hardly a household name. I was introduced through an article in YES! Magazine to Dr. Ostrum's research on "Governing the Commons: The Evolution of Institutions for Collective Action". I was excited because it resolved Garrett Hardin's Tragedy of the Commons.

David was struck by, and enlightened me to, the evolutionary implications of what he and Dr. Ostrum came to call the Eight Core Design Principles for organizing every kind of human group endeavor. You would be quite correct in assuming this sounds pretty important. This technology will play a critical role in the decades to come and will be a feature of the movement I am.

In 2015, my brother, Robert was gathering family input for my father's eulogy. It took me a restless night of self-introspection to come up with a response that befit the role Dad played in my life. I told Robert: "If it is possible, as some believe, to choose one's parents, then that choice was the best decision I ever made". It is almost comical to say that I had stumbled unwittingly into the spiritual universe! (Goosebumps!)

I can assure you that I had no concept of the importance, provenance, and poignancy of those spirit-inspired words, until I learned about the power of postulates and basic workings of the spiritual world. It is astonishing to look back at the myriad other small instances of these connections over the course of a lifetime.

This past week I was speaking with my best friend from High School, Jérôme Glain. In fact, I was staying with him at his family's home when The Accident happened. For fifty years on and off, I had been trying to track him down and he was trying to find me. Finally, we succeeded, just a few months ago. We now chat every other week by Zoom, picking our friendship back up seamlessly as if time made no difference. I could not possibly have foreseen what he would share with me this morning after I opened up to him about my spiritual awakening.

When I asked him if he had ever felt a strange connection or calling. His answer was "Yes". "Frequently [he said], throughout my life when I am talking with someone, I grow really tall and I look down on them and this extreme peace and elation overwhelm me." I pressed him further to describe this experience: "It's like being in a room full of a really bright light. The light is so bright that I think it may consume me. It is too big for me to wrap my head around it…. Also, there's a thing about time, I feel that I have all the time in the world because there is no time. I call it "angel time". Like us getting together after 50 years. It is like it happened yesterday."

However, you experience such a revelation, goosebumps, a whack on the head, a gentle inclination, stop and heed the moment! Let that thought, whatever it may be, become intention. The specific intention becomes, like a dream, a portal into the spiritual realm. You have been given a key to the door ahead of you. Go ahead. Open it. In the spiritual dimension duality has no claim on you— there is no good and no evil, no wrong and no right, no heaven and no hell. Pass through the door ahead, and the next, and the next.

The sooner you practice listening to that inner voice, the better you will get at it. Your rewards await you.

Listen also to the inner voices of others. I am thankful for the compassion and wisdom of my wife's oldest brother, Chuck. Thank you for teaching me to see with new eyes and leading me to a compassionate acceptance of The Accident. To my new Teacher, Raymond, who reminded me of the words Leonard Cohen wrote for the song "Anthem": "There is a crack, a crack in everything… That's how the light gets in".

"Acquire inner peace and thousands around you will find salvation."

—Saint Seraphim of Sarov (1759-1833)
Russian monk and mystic

My pilgrimage is almost over, surrounded by friends and teachers to guide me, restored in my relationship with my Heart, strengthened with love and forgiveness, I am now completely free of the greatest fear I had during those years searching in "the wilderness", the fear that my heart was becoming encased in a thick armor threatening to stifle all love. Peace and its partner Serenity are open to me now. I listened. Eventually, I heeded. I forgave myself. And, finally, today I truly grasp that without forgiveness there is no Peace, No Serenity.

The title of the essay "Love thy neighbor as thy self" actually had to work in the reverse order. It was easy to love my neighbor, but it took 50 years for me to accept, forgive and love myself again. (Goosebumps!)

Every thought or intention can become a postulate. I contend that if you do so with bad intentions nothing good will come of it, least of all for you. On the other hand, if your intentions, or postulates, are positive, by which I mean full with loving-kindness and intended to do good, good will increase in your life as much as it will in the lives of others close to you. When you work in a group full of loving-kindness, you exponentially increase the spread loving-kindness in your life and in the lives of others.

You have the power to change Yourself and, in the shelter of each other, the power to amplify the change, joining with others to do good *For the Good of All, NOW!*

Heed the moments! Love Yourself! Love Your Neighbor! To Life!

Please connect with David Currie by email at
dandmlcurrie@gmail.com

FALLEN INTO MY LAP

Gregor Hočevar
ORBIT™ Coaching Client

I run a family business. We work in a construction field, not just any construction but in a special specific niche. We install stainless steel chimney pipes. It's a very unique business which includes a lot of different knowledge that you have to gain to make it work. I have to be a mortar, climber, engineer, electrician, roofer, psychologist and a lot more.

My dad started the business back in 1994 and he was just about to retire. As my company expanded, I needed a new co-worker. There was just too much work to do and I couldn't handle it anymore so I needed help. I started to look everywhere. And my company is well-known throughout country and exists for more than 25 years we gained a lot of contact. I started to call each and every business partner or a person that I knew could help me about to find a new co-worker. And if you can imagine there were a lot of numbers and a lot of phone calls to me and guess what I had no luck. I started to ask each and every person wherever I went if they knew someone who could work for me. Nothing happened. Then my friends called me and said he has a guy who can help me.

I said okay give me his phone number and I'll call him make him meeting and we will discuss about the work. He said he could do job for me and I said okay and told him he has due two weeks trial. He began to work next day I immediately saw he's probably not the one I was looking for but I didn't have any choice. I could see he's not as agile and dexterous like I wanted him to be. When the second week was about to end, I came back home and I knew I will have to say to him in 2 days that he's not the one. That same day I was working on my papers and I opened my email. I was scrolling through and one email caught my attention. It was a message from a guy named Ismet. He wrote To Me: Hi my name is Ismet. I come from Bosnia. 24 years old. I'm installing stainless steel chimney pipes for four years now. I'm looking for a new job do you have something for me.

Now that's might sound normal, but the guy sends me an e-mail at exactly perfect time when I needed him. And not only that. he is from another country speaks another language. It's not a language barrier for me because I know hot speak his language but he doesn't speak my language. and I asked him how did you find me and he said I typed in Google something about chimneys in Slovenia and the first page that popped out was yours. I immediately sent an email and responded, like he had *Fallen Into My Lap*.

What's the options that something like that happens. If we just consider that in the whole area (not only my country) maybe 50 company are specialized in working/installing with stainless steel chimney pipes.

Actually, work and has four years of experience that's call me it's just amazing. If we calculate options my opinion is that I would sooner win a lotto ticket then have found him, but I didn't find him he found me. He is just a complete package, young, experienced and willing to work.

I didn't hesitate. I called him right away and told him to come. Where will I sleep and I said you will sleep in my house just come and I will give you two weeks of probation but as soon as she picked up first machine, I knew he's the guy.

Please email Gregor Hočevar at hocevar.gregor@gmail.com for more information and purchase his book on Amazon, *Treat Your Clients Like Royalty: Improve the Client Experience and Dramatically Increase Your Income.*

MY ARTHRITIS PAIN

Thomas Hurley
ORBIT™ Coaching Client

Arthritis has been a problem for me for over 12 years. Then 10 years ago, I had my left ankle fused because of the pain the arthritis caused in the ankle. The arthritis was not constant and moved around my body, some of the bad spots were the knees and the shoulders. One and a half years ago I had stem cell therapy in my left knee, my right shoulder, and my blood and the doctor said I would have needed a replacement in six months.

I did not want any replacement because I needed both knees and both shoulders to be replaced meaning many operations and years of recovery. The pain caused depression and the inability to do many things.

Two months ago, I started taking Raymond Aaron's courses and began learning how to postulate. Thanks to his courses and learning how to postulate, I have now got rid of my arthritis. The pain has gone from my body. Yesterday was the first day for many years that I got up off the floor without using a chair, the couch or any other help up off the floor.

A week ago, I stayed up past midnight which I had not done for years and I got up early the next morning. This has been miraculous for me.

Please visit Thomas Hurley's website at http://Personalmoney management.club for more information or email him directly at tombhur@gmail.com.

Thomas Hurley has written a book, *Personal Money Management: Methods of Self-Improvement* and you can purchase a copy of his book on Amazon.

RIDE TO RICHES

Pat Ramsay
ORBIT™ Coaching Client

By the age of 24, in my 9 to 5 job, I achieved a supervisor position and I felt like I could achieve anything! I began to look for something new and came across an opportunity to fulfill a need in the transportation industry. I continued to work my supervisor role while getting my transportation company off the ground. It took 6 months to figure out the logistics and financing of the business I was starting from scratch before I was able to leave my day job. It was remarkable the success I achieved in a short amount of time. My new company was thriving in unbelievable ways. To add to my blessings my wife had just told me that she was pregnant with our first child.

But it was not always like this...

For a couple years, I drudged in my 9 to 5 job, and knew there had to be something else in life. It was not long after the first year in my current transportation business that the rate of pay was drastically reduced. With the rates being cut and now a child on the way, I needed to find a way to survive and provide for my growing family. I was in despair and wondered how I could endure this situation.

I knew from past experience that there is a solution to every puzzle and a way out of every box, it was just a question of where to find the answer. I could create something more because I had already made big changes in the past. I recognized there were greater opportunities available to me.

It was not until the world came crashing down on me and my family that I had the clarity and the courage to create a postulate. In that moment, my postulate was to achieve my first million dollars within a year. I was able to change my old belief like I changed clothes it all came off and I put something new on. This was the best thing that could have happened to me.

I immediately started to look for opportunities that presented themselves that would allow me to create my postulate. The next morning, I found an opportunity to grow my transportation business in another city and so I packed up and all our belongings, sold the house, and moved to a new city. When this occurred, I knew deep inside this was right and even though the path was not clear. Opposition was futile. This gave me the courage to take the leap of faith because the alternative was to endure hardship and struggle. Suffering was not acceptable because I had just tolerated that same feeling in my 9 to 5 job.

I had to be separated from my wife for three months because I couldn't find housing at the new location. My wife was so close to giving birth that I decided I would rent a room in a house until adequate housing could be found for our growing family. Once I moved to the city, I started working 120 hours a week to get the business going. I was in constant communication with my wife as she was so close to giving birth and I had so much pressure and stress because I didn't want to miss the birth of our first child. She was staying an eight-hour drive away with no opportunity for flights. Then the call came in late February, I just finished my work day and went to bed at 11pm, it was 2 am, my wife was in labour. I had just a few hours of sleep and had to start making the trek in the worst snowstorm that winter. It took 10 hours to arrive at the hospital and the whole time all I could think about was being there to witness the birth of our first child. I made it, and when I held my son for the first time, it gave me even more inspiration. I could only stay a few days and went back to continue with the business and find a suitable home for my family.

I found a small rental house and moved my family two weeks later. There was not much to rent at all in this city and the only thing I could find was a house that had interior walls colored peach! The new place became known as the "Peach Pit". It was an extremely difficult time because I was in a new city where I knew no one and had no family nearby for any support. Immediately, opportunities began to present themselves, in retrospect those opportunities did not show a clear path but my desire to succeed and achieve sprang me into action. I was able to purchase a house within 6 months after moving into the peach pit. There was so much that was going on in my life at the time the postulate faded into the background. Six months later, while looking at a monthly income statement I discovered that I had achieved my postulate. I had created $1,000,000 dollars! Upon realization of this postulate, it was only three years later that I grew my company 5 ½ times that size. I was recognized for being the youngest person ever, in my current location within the transportation sector, to achieve this.

Upon reflection, the postulate allowed me to continue through any and all obstacles that came within my path. Looking back if the pay decrease did not happen the postulate would not have been created and the $1,000,000 dollars would not have happened like it did.

Connect with Patrick Ramsay at transitionmaster.com and also purchase his book on Amazon, *The Authorities - Patrick Ramsay.*

YOUTH IS PERFECT FOR POSTULATING

Debra Parks Root PhD, ND
ORBIT™ Coaching Client

When Raymond asked me to write this chapter on postulates, those thoughts that come from our true selves, I thought back on my life.

How did I get to where I am now? How did I achieve all the successes I have achieved?

How was I able to sing with some of the greatest musicians in the world as lead female singer for the Ginger Baker and Friends' Band (World famous drummer Ginger Baker of Cream, Blind Faith, Air Force). I was also female singer for Emerson Lake and Palmer 's American "3" Tour.

How did I become a successful model and actress?

How did I win Miss Oklahoma UN?

How did I invent and patent a food product and create a successful worldwide business around that invention? How did my invention become the best-selling new product on QVC?

How did I successfully homeschool all four of my children? Allowing my oldest daughter to attended Harvard University (and Oxford University) where she graduated Magna Cum Laude. Now she's in her last year of achieving her PhD at the Ecole Normale Superieure (ENS) in Paris, France.

How was I able to write and publish the book "Homeschool to Harvard"? For more information visit HomeschooltoHarvard.com

How am I inventing other patented products and creating successful businesses around those inventions?

How do I create and develop television shows? What got me to this point? (If you would like to see photos of the above—please go to DebraRoot.com)

Postulates!

I realized my postulate ability started back when I was 13 years old.

That's when my parents became Amway distributors. With any good multi-level marketing company, it is important to teach members how to set goals, how to achieve those goals and how to think positively. Throughout my teenage years, my parents took me around to many different conventions, where I enjoyed listening to numerous positive thinking speakers.

Whenever in the car, especially on the drive to church every Sunday, we would listen to the recordings of different positive thinking speakers as they discussed success, goals, making money, health, achievement, working hard, being the best you can be, etc. I drank it up. I thoroughly enjoyed listening to these amazing orators speaking about how to better my life, how to create and live the life of my dreams. At 13, I was a sponge and I loved hearing how to create and have the best life I could. I'm very grateful that my parents taught me this at such a young age. I know this is what fueled my amazing and wonderful life. I realize how blessed I was to have such wonderful parents Ralph and Martha Parks. **They also taught me that I was worthy of those goals.**

At that time, I was taught that I was just setting goals and learning how to achieve them. Not until I met Raymond Aaron and took his amazing Mulberry Hill Gang webinar, did I realize I had been postulating when setting those goals. Funny, my definition of a Postulate is–if a prayer and a goal got together and had a baby–that baby is a postulate!

Sitting down to write this chapter for Raymond, I remembered that at the tender young age of 13, I had written out my first postulate list. I wondered if I could find the first goalsetting pages I had ever written down, essentially my very first written postulates. I searched through several big boxes in the back of my closet.

Low and behold, there was my list, my first draft of the rest of my life, in my cute little girl handwriting.

Looking at this decades old postulate list, I had found the starting place of my wonderful, fulfilling and amazing life. I felt like I was looking at my life's map. This map showed me the directions to go, but not the millions of serendipitous pathways God would take me on to arrive at those Postulates.

These delicious, strange and remarkable pathways lead me to exotic places around the world, and allowed me to accomplish my hearts desires. I did things that I could never have dreamed of. That's one of the most amazing parts about postulates. At 13 years of age, I could not have possibly foreseen the immense variety of experiences I was blessed to go through (and will keep doing in the future). At the time, I didn't write down exact postulates. I just wrote down general desires: snow ski, waterski, sing, beach house, Hawaii, plane, diamonds, etc. Now with life experience I am able to focus my postulates exactly how I want them.

Postulates are not taught in school. I was blessed to have the ability to learn from Raymond Aaron and some of the greatest success thinking minds, speeches, books and videos. This changed everything for a young girl from Oklahoma, USA. Without this positive influence in my life, I do not know where I would have ended up or what I would have achieved. Postulates made all of the difference in my life. I even make my children read some of the goal setting books that I feasted on as a child: *How to Win Friends and Influence People*—Dale Carnegie, *Believe It and Achieve It*—Brian Tracy, *Rich Dad Poor Dad*—Robert Kiyosaki, *The 7 Habits of Highly Effective People*—Stephen Covey, *Think and Grow Rich*—Napoleon Hill, *The Power of Positive Thinking*—Norman Vincent Peale, *Live your Dreams*—Les Brown, *Chicken Soup for the Parents Soul*—Raymond Aaron, *You were Born Rich*—Bob Proctor.

What did these Postulates at the age of 13 do for me?

1. Postulates gave me direction.

If you look at the horizon, it is huge. It is limitless. There is no quantifier for how and where to move. It's too big. However, with postulates, I have a focus to look for what I want in my life on the horizon that points me in the correct direction to move forward towards my destination from the thought process of my postulate. Postulates are the compass to our dream life. Otherwise, I am a boat without a rudder being controlled by the current and waves.

2. I can see where I am—kind of like a child's game of "Hot & Cold".

When I am nearing my postulate, I am warm/happier. When I am missing my postulate, I am cold /unhappy. The hot or warm may feel like good emotions and happy positive feelings whereas the cold may make you feel lost, disappointed, too hard, and too many problems. What a wonderful gage our feelings give us to help us create the life of our dreams.

3. I have direction when I am moving towards my Postulates.

My Postulate is my direction. Then God puts the perfect impulses on my path and I can listen and move towards those impulses to manifestation. It's like I'm tracking my goals in the forest, eagerly searching for clues that bring me closer to my postulates. Those divine impulses trigger my behaviors and thoughts to move me toward my postulates. If I am driving from Las Vegas to Los Angeles, I know to head west for 270 miles and I'll arrive. Therefore, when I stop in Barstow, I don't get frustrated and give up on my trip because I am not in Los Angeles yet—I know to keep heading west and in another two hours, I will be in Los Angeles. We need to understand that our postulates take time to manifest just like that drive to LA. We don't just give up after a few setbacks. We must believe in our mind that our postulate IS and no matter what the circumstances facing us in the moment, we know that it will all work out for our postulates. No worrying only believing.

4. Aim for the moon and touch the stars!

This really happened for me. At 13, I wrote down specific goals, wants, dreams, wishes and desires. At that time, I didn't realize these were postulates. What I didn't know then was how amazing and glorious the manifestations of those postulates would actually turn out to be—thousands of times better than expected. I dreamed so big and I achieved all of my dreams. My child me, wanted to dream big, wanted to use my imagination to become anything I wanted. Listening to all the success speakers over those formative years allowed me to keep my goal setting postulates and know I can be, do or have anything I put my mind to. As Brian Tracy said, "All successful people are big dreamers." That makes children innately successful. It is adulthood that takes some peoples dreams away.

5. I learned what I do want and what I don't want.

This is huge. At the young age of 13, I didn't have much life experience and didn't know what my real preferences were. Over the years we learn our preferences through trial and error. This is an amazing part of life. Setting a desire and achieving it—than realizing I didn't really like it as much as I thought I would. I always wanted to live on the beach in Malibu, California. Well, I achieved that only to find out that living on the ocean was very difficult at times. Sand was everywhere in the house. Everything rusted so fast. Living on Pacific Coast Highway was very stressful especially if you have kids and dogs. The fires in Malibu were a constant worry and it is very loud during storms when the waves would actually break on our deck. I found it not as glamours as it seems. Achieving that goal help me understand my likes and dislikes.

6. Expectations versus Postulates.

At 13 years old I had huge, fearless, expectations of the life I wanted to live. I wasn't clouded by stress, life, bills, debt, peer pressure, the aches and pain of aging, disappointing failures, and negative lifestyles. I was a blank canvas wanting to enjoy my life's unfolding. Looking towards the future with eyes wide open, eagerly waiting for life to happen. My imagination was my driving force. I expected the best life ever! I was my own superhero with superpowers to create my own amazing life! Nothing was going to stop me.

Perhaps it was easier for me to start at such a young age. I have seen so many adults give up on their dreams. Their exceptions lower every year of their lives, because they dwell upon their many failures and the negative reality they choose to look at. Complaining becomes their mantra.

Imagine an archery target with the center red circle and many circles around that center. Most people get caught up in the outside circles never believing they can reach the target. They just keep going around in circles barely alive, bored, tired, sad, unfulfilled and confused. They never believed in themselves enough to set the goals for what they really want. So, they got stuck circling around the target, complaining about how horrible their lives are. Expecting less and less every year until they die.

If you're going to shoot an arrow you are going to focus and aim for the center target. It may take hundreds of arrows/tries to achieve your target. But you don't give up the first time you miss. You keep trying. This is what everyone knows and understands if you wish to excel in archery. It's the same in life—you need to focus then aim for your targeted postulates, dreams or goals. Knowing that you will get closer to your goals as you miss. But you keep trying again and again. But most adults seem to think if they fail once at their dreams—they can never achieve them. Then embarrassed, they give up on their dreams to go on to living a life of mediocrity and boredom.

7. Postulates are the fuel to my future.

Fuel is energy. Energy gets you going and keeps you moving. Time is always moving forward, therefore time is energy—your fuel. You don't want to waste your time. You try to use your time wisely to get the most value for every moment. Money is another type of fuel for your postulates. You're not going to waste your money on useless things that don't benefit you? You will use your money to your full potential. You will use your time and money to help you propel yourself towards your postulates. Postulates give you the ability to get things done as they arrive in your now. When an opportunity that aligns with your postulate comes along, you will happily and excitedly follow that opportunity. And say no to the non-aligning goal opportunity that doesn't ring your bells. You will know the difference between what opportunities will help you achieve your postulates and what opportunities that will not help you to your postulates. Remember your time is like your money. If you put off what needs to be done now—you lose money and time. A fire must always have fuel otherwise it will die. Similar to your postulates. Always stoke the fire of your dreams, and give your dreams fuel to live on.

As Pablo Picasso said "Only put off until tomorrow what you are willing to die having left undone."

8. Anything I put my mind to!

Wow those are amazing words! My mind is my place of dreams, imagination, postulates, and creation. Therefore, if I put my mind to it—I can achieve it. Jesus Christ said

"Whatever you ask in Prayer, believe that you have received it, and it will be yours." Children not only believe in their prayers and dreams—they become what they want in their imaginations. Example, A little girl wants to be an astronaut, she than uses her imagination to act and become an astronaut. She actually becomes that astronaut in the international space station. Floating around in her imagination, enjoying every minute of her space odyssey, until dinner is ready.

9. "And she lived happily ever after!"

Children's fairy tale books have gotten a bad rap lately. For the correct reasons: no diversity, passive damsels in distressed that can only be saved by a prince that ultimately, she must marry, etc. However, if you look at my life, the young me that Postulated those wonderful dreams on my list—got those dreams. My life is the best fairy tale ever. Yes "and she lived happily ever after!" does exist. This was my fairy tale that I am living right now. But I am living Happily NOW! Not just after. I learned that from watching my own children. Children are innately happy. Always knowing everything will work out for them. They live in their imagination and allow their dreams and possibilities to move them forward. Not like adults that dwell on their past failures and present situation—letting the negative reality of their or other people's lives hold them back like chains to a past illusion.

10. "Gonna Get list."

I have achieved almost everything on my 13-year-old "Gonna Get list". I have either gone there, bought that, done that, lived there, or traveled there. I am so very blessed. What I found most interesting was that I had known I wanted four children at that early age. How did I know I wanted two boys and two girls?

Is that an intention I came into my life with (again quoting Raymond Aaron from Mulberry Hill Gang)? I am now happily divorced. That marriage brought me my four beautiful, perfect, amazing, intelligent, children that I am grateful for very day. I also realized that my four phenomenal children are by far my most amazing accomplishments in my life. Daily, I realize how blessed I am that they came to me and I am honored to be their mother. I guess I always knew, I wanted to be the best mother possible. And I hope I have been.

My Postulate list from decades ago, shows me how important requesting postulates really is. My postulates have been creating my life. The life I have already lived, my amazing moments right now and now moving forward, I am happily anticipating the phenomenal rest of my life. I feel like Postulates are my "Genie in the lamp" any wish is granted to me. But I get unlimited wishes, not just three! Isn't that amazing? We all have the ability to be Aladdin and wish for anything and know it will happen—if we believe and are happy and gratefully living our lives.

Now, with Raymond Aaron as my mentor, I'm creating new postulates that are wonderfully unfolding in my life now and I am eager to enjoy. These new postulates are in line with the me of now—today. And now with the maturity and wisdom of decades of successes and failures, I look forward to postulating even more and listening to the impulses that God gives me to follow the correct path to joyfully receive the beautiful sprinkling of miracles that heaven showers upon me daily. I just have to be happy and appreciate all that I am, all that I have lived, and all that will be—and everything I want will magically flow to me.

DUMB THINGS I GOTTA GET
1 skis poles bindings
2 water bed
3 new wardrobe
4 model school
5 bike
6 moped
7 moon boots
8 cowboy boots
9 indian earths
10 windsurf board
11 water ski
12 ski boat

DUMB THINGS I GOTTA DO
1 wet suit
2 mountain climbing stuff
3 big dog
4 own phone
5 money to give
6 weigh 130
7 read at 14,000 words/min
8 healthy skin
9 muscle tone
10 uncellulited skin
11 Wet man II
12 4 KID'S 2 girls

DUMB THINGS I GOTTA DO
1 "64" con Vette!
2 beach house
3 new curtains
4 new furniture
5 STEREO
6 motorcycle
7 good tennis racket
8 pearl necklaces
9 ski outfit
10 Pepperdine U.
11 steel string guitar
12 electric guitar

DUMB THINGS I GOTTA DO
1 sailboat
2 catamaran!
3 170 ft yacht!
4 go to Europe ski
5 scuba diving stuff
6 AFS for a year
7 Cruiser that travels
8 Crew member direct
9 Invitable Prelude
10 condos all over
11 beach, ski resorts
12 Handsome Hunk

DUMB THINGS I GOTTA DO
1 diamond earrings
2 diamond ring
3 Portable cassette recorder
4 MAID for mom
5 boyfriend for Kitty
6 jet ski
7 parachute
8 hang glider
9 plane Lear Jet
10 pilot lessons
11 surf board
12 school for teens

DUMB THINGS I GOTTA DO
1 banjo
2 drums
3 harp
4 harmonica
5 fiddle
6 xylophone
7 condo in Hawaii
8 islands of Hawaii
9 backpacking equip.
10 4 wheel truck.
11 electric car.
12 plantation style house

For more information on Debra Root, go to DebraRoot.com

SUMMON BILLIONAIRES TO YOU

Raj Singh
ORBIT™ Coaching Client

Upon browsing the Internet, I saw an event where I could finally meet one of my hero's… the unconventional billionaire, Sir Richard Branson. And, it was at the legendary and iconic Playboy Mansion in Los Angeles, which many young men dream of visiting. To complete the trifecta of reasons why I just had to attend… it was a charity gala event for a great cause. Eureka! It was destiny.

As I'm at this black-tie event, meeting A-List Hollywood celebrities in the backstage VIP area of the mansion, I see Sir Richard Branson walking towards my direction from my right side. I proceeded to take my cell phone out of my pocket to capture this moment, forever. Then I notice walking towards me from the opposite direction, my left side, is P. Diddy. Now I'm hurriedly launching the camera app on my phone.

Both of these business moguls stop walking, as they meet up with each other, about a foot away from the exact spot I am standing, just behind me. I could reach out and touch them both. As I'm taking a selfie of me with them right behind me, I can hear Diddy speaking.

Diddy said something like "Hello Mr. Branson. My name is Sean Combs, and I'm grateful for all the work your foundations have been doing in the world, thank you." As they speak more, I am in awe that I just stumbled upon, by chance, the spot where these 2 ultra-successful global superstars just happened to cross paths for apparently the very 1st time.

This story gets even better/crazier. And yes, the pictures of this are on my social media.

It wasn't until the next day, when I was in the airport to fly home, that I looked at my phone, and what I saw caused me to almost drop the phone out of my hands in shock. Something had jumped out to me on the background of my phone screen. It was my vision board. On my vision board has a celebrity section of celebs I will meet in the future.

In that section I saw Sir Richard Branson, of course. I also saw Diddy there. But the part that had me feeling like I was in an episode of The Twilight Zone was when I realized the placement of both of their pictures on my vision board... they were the only ones touching each other!

Branson was scheduled to be there at the event. Diddy was not. What are the chances, in all time and space, that I would just happen to be there, at the same time the both of them were, as they coincidentally met there for the very 1st time, and I am a foot away from them, as they both came to me? This is one of many experiences I have had, and my coaching clients have also had, that prove that magical things can happen when you have and believe in a vision board, and manifesting, and postulating what you desire to the Universe. Did I cause those 2 mega-giant celebrities to meet for the 1st time just because I was there?

The better question is how can you apply this to your life to have amazing and magical things happen to you as well. Raymond Aaron has been a mentor of mine for over a decade and I am grateful for his teachings of the spiritual world. As my clients and I continue to annually update our vision board, our audio affirmations of our own voice, and our dream vision movie, we continue to see the unbelievable, and what seems impossible, results that follow.

Coming from a technical IT background, I know this can all sound a bit woo-woo. So does the idea of Wi-Fi, but I'm wise enough to take advantage of it anyway. After all, I'd rather be seen as cray-cray and be successful, than to be seen as cool and be broke-minded.

———————

Raj in Hindi means "King," so it is no coincidence that he is truly living a life dedicated to serving and inspiring others, while treating his clients like royalty. He is an award-winning author, TEDx speaker, serial entrepreneur, and global rockstar, as the lead singer of a Caribbean band, that jet sets around the world for fun every week, since leaving Corporate America over a decade ago because of his investments working for him. He serves on the executive board of Toastmasters Int'l, non-profits, spiritual groups, and was chosen to be the honorary Grand Marshal of his city. When you follow him on social media you will see that he is consistently flying on private jets, wining and dining with A-List celebrities, giving back to 3rd world countries in need, but most of all, always makes time for his family and friends.

But it wasn't always like this. Money was a big issue as a child of divorced parents. Working in the IT field, he just knew he was destined for more. Now his mission is to teach people like you, how to generate multiple streams of passive income, like he did, through his proprietary "5M" system, to create financial freedom, so you can truly experience life to the fullest. Interested? Learn more about King Raj's experience and wisdom, read his book titled *"The Authorities: Control Money Before Money Controls You"*

For more information on Raj Singh, go to www.TheKingRaj.com

HOLIDAY INN REWARDS

Karen-Marie Siyanbola-Ellington
ORBIT™ Coaching Client

I had registered for Raymond Aaron's 10-10-10 Program, the book writing bootcamp being held at Holiday Inn, Yorkdale (Toronto, Canada). Being from Oakville, at least an hour's drive on the highway, I checked the weather report for the next three days. Sure enough, snow was predicted for the morning commute on the last of the three days. Should I or shouldn't I book to stay overnight? I had invested money into the program that wasn't really mine to spend but this was my 'Leap of Faith,' and I was making a commitment to my dream. I told myself, I want to make sure that I am there early Thursday morning, so I will book to stay overnight. It will be worth it; I will be rewarded for my effort. So, I booked it.

Little did I know what would happen next. I made the call to book and was asked if I was interested in signing up for the Rewards program, after all it was free to join. I said yes, not knowing or expecting much. The primary purpose was to market the hotel by word of mouth and receive some perks in return. I could only get the advertised discount for the room if I joined. So I did, "What the heck I thought." I was then passed on to Rewards Manager to 'get the spiel, as they say. She started thanking me and then proceeded to tell me that this year, the hotel chain is celebrating its 70th anniversary. So for becoming a Rewards member, I am being offered a holiday package of 5 nights, 4 days at any of 20 destinations chosen and listed in the USA for a total cost of $279 US. Upon checking in, I have the choice of getting back the total cost in cash or $179 US in cash along with 20,000 points towards another stay.

The evening I checked in, my discounted standard, 2 double bed room was upgraded to a King size bed / sitting room on the Rewards Floor. I was then given a complimentary invitation to a reception being held in a private Dining Room for Rewards Members only. Previously I had imagined having a nice dinner in the hotel's dining area later on after class, not wanting to go off site again, once settled. Then the invitation came for the group to have dinner together and I said yes, picturing this vision. When I heard that the group was heading off site for dinner, I was of two minds to go. Then I checked into my room....

I was ushered into the smaller, private dining room and offered wine or soft beverage of choice, hors devours and roast beef served on top of yorkshire pudding. The other people in the room were all from two companies. I was the Lone Ranger. I ended up talking with a very pleasant woman, telling her I was at a writer's workshop as "an award winning author with an upcoming book titled, *Turn NO Into YES, 10 Ways to Transform Your Outlook on Life*. She lit up like a lightbulb and proceeded to tell me about her life, where she is at and where she wants to be. We talked for over half an hour and exchanged email addresses. She is very interested in getting my book and happens to be the Executive Assistant to the CEO of Bombardier. They were there to broker a deal with Mitsubishi. I went to bed very satisfied.

Please connect with Karen-Marie Siyanbola-Ellington by email at ka.siyanbola@gmail.com

I'M GOING TO HELP THEM FIGURE IT OUT!

Ray Wilson
ORBIT™ Coaching Client

I have to do something. I don't know what to do. I need someone to help me figure out what to do. When I grow up, I'm going to help people figure out what to do.

That is what I said when I was 8 years old. I don't remember what the situation was. All I remember is that I needed to help others figure out what to do when I grew up.

I had totally forgot about that incident until one year, decades later, I was being interviewed for a book and the interviewer asked me how did you get into what you are into today? It was then that I remembered the promise I had made as a little boy.

At that time there were no such thing as a life coach or a personal development coach. It never occurred to me that I would be the Results Coach.

I was a quiet individual as a youngster. I grew up with my stepfather who was always yelling at me to shut up, so I was a quiet person. As I was growing up, my attitude was to talk when I had something important to say. Most of the time I really didn't think I had anything important to say.

When I was a little boy, my grandmother told me I was going to be a minister. I found that interesting because I wasn't even part of a religious organization. I didn't even go to church when I was young. I had no idea what a minister actually did. I didn't realize they guided people on how to live a better life. I did not even set my foot in a church in until my early twenties. However, being a minister never even cross my mind.

I didn't notice until I was much older that as a teenager, I always advising my friends. We'd play a game of basketball and then a group of guys would be hanging around me as I advised them on how to address challenges they were having or giving them advice on how to improve their life.

When I was a teenager, I was always reading personal development books. Personal development was introduced to me by my father who gave me the book "Grow Rich with the Peace of Mind" by Napoleon Hill. I was reluctant to read the book. It took two years before I ever open and read the book. It changed my life!

I grew up as an angry young man because I experienced racism at its worst. I grew up in crime infested neighborhoods and lived in poverty and I had to navigate through all of that. Nobody could help me because all people around me were in the same condition. I kept on reading personal development books and little by little, I was changing.

People who know me now don't believe that I use to curse every other word. I kept reading the personal development books and one day I was looking in the mirror and said to myself I don't recognize you. I had changed. I had change from an angry young man to a positive person. I didn't curse anymore. I focused on making positive changes instead of hurting myself and others.

Eventually I went to college and graduated. As I enter into my new career again I experienced extreme levels of racism and unfair treatment. The funny thing is my colleagues who did not experience this level of injustice were coming to me discussing their frustrations with their job and life and were asking for advice.

The first job I obtained after graduating from college was working, for one of the largest government jurisdictions in the United States, as an internal auditor. My primary responsibility was to go into organizations to identify their problems and provide them with recommendations to help them resolve the issues. Little did I know this was preparing me to fulfill the postulate I had made at 8 years old.

During that time, I joined Toastmasters International because I wanted to improve my communication skills. I was always ready to give a speech even when I wasn't scheduled or placed on the agenda. The quiet guy was not so quiet anymore because I had something to say.

All of my speeches were on personal development even though I didn't plan it that way. It had an impact on the members of the group. They would share with me how the subject matter and the message delivered helped them to address a challenge they were dealing with in their life. People began to ask me to come speak to their organizations. Eventually I was asked to speak at conferences.

The organizer at one conference I was scheduled speak at asked me did I have a book to sell. I replied no. It never crossed my mind to write a book. The organizer said you need something to sell. And so, I created a book titled „Create a Better You." From that book, I began to receive more speaking requests.

While I enjoyed speaking, I enjoyed helping people one-on-one with their specific challenges more. I was always coaching individuals who worked for me and my co-workers would come to me requesting guidance on addressing various issues. I was really effective in helping them and I really enjoyed it. So, I began coaching people, but I had no structure or framework for coaching. I didn't even know that there was a profession or training to become a coach. At the time there was not. However, I was the internal auditor who was going into organizations to identify problems and come up with recommendations to address those problems. The auditing of these organizations provided me with a structure and a framework that I converted it into my coaching.

It wasn't until years later that the profession of coaching came into my radar. I had always gone to personal development workshops, but I never heard about a workshop for coaches. Then one day I attended a seminar where the speaker offered a certified training program on transformation and Leadership coaching. As he was describing it, I jumped up and headed for the sign-up table. I was the first one to sign up for the program.

After that I continued learning about coaching others and obtaining other certifications in coaching. Then I started developing coaching products that have been extremely effective in helping people overcome their obstacles and achieving their goals and attaining successful outcomes.

In the Decades of coaching and mentoring individuals, I never realized this is what I was destined to do until that interviewer ask me the question how did you get into what you are into today? What motivates you to help other people overcome obstacles and guide them into obtaining successful outcomes.

The eight-year-old boy said "I have to do something. I don't know what to do. I need someone to help me figure out what to do. When I grow up, I'm going to help people figure out what to do.

What a postulate!

As a Certified High Performance Coach and Certified Leadership and Transformation Coach, I would love to work with you. I can be contacted at www.ObstacleCrusher.Com for a consult or free strategy session.

SECTION 2

MORE *POSTULATE LIKE A PRO* STORIES

GETTING TO THE CASTLE

Emma Aaron

My very first job after high school was as a tutor for three children living in a castle in Tipperary, Ireland. One weekend, I was taking the bus back to the castle from Dublin and was trying to arrange for someone to pick me up at the bus stop.

No one that I knew was available to drive me.

It was getting near the end of my two-hour journey back to Tipperary and the sun had already set. There were no streetlights in that village and I had heavy bags to carry, so walking home was not an option. I made up my mind that a solution would appear.

A few minutes later, the bus stopped suddenly at a huge empty field in the middle of nowhere. The bus driver called over to me and explained that he had driven past the last stop because he thought the bus was empty. I was the only passenger left. He turned the bus around and headed back for the stop.

Since the sun was down, he asked if someone would be waiting there to pick me up. I described that I was staying at the other end of the village and hadn't been able to get a ride. He looked very concerned. I decided to make a bold move and ask if he would be able to drive me home rather than back to the bus stop. I quickly tried to explain where the castle was, but he did not know the area well and he mumbled something about not going off his route. I gave up and went back to my seat.

It was dark, so I didn't bother to look out the window as we drove back. The bus pulled over again a few minutes later and the driver asked if I knew my way home from there. I looked out the bus window and saw that HE HAD STOPPED RIGHT IN FRONT OF THE CASTLE DRIVEWAY!

Connect with Emma Aaron at help@aaron.com.

CRACKING THE CODE

Alejandra Diaz Mercado

Since I was a child, I was aware that impossible coincidences often happened around me. They also seemed to follow me like a moody outdoor cat, showing up wherever and whenever they wanted.

There were the instances where I would think of a specific movie I wanted to watch, only to turn on the TV a couple hours later as it was about to start, or coming up with a question I needed to ask a certain friend seconds before my mother announced the call on the landline was for me, from no other than the friend I wanted to ask the question to.

Much to my horror and dismay there were also other instances where I happened to predict calamities such as the exact day our dog escaped never to be found, deaths in my family and people tripping and falling right in front of me shortly after I had a vision of them tripping and falling.

I recently had one of those unfortunate experiences at the gym.

Upon entering the training facility, I was denied access to towel service for the first time in 7 years. This put me in a foul mood. After leaving my belongings in the locker room I proceeded to the elliptical machine where, as expected, I started sweating profusely. By then, not only were my pores exuding sweat but also anger.

I was blowing things out of proportion with my inner dialogue and because of my past experiences I knew I needed to put a halt to that *before something happened*. But before I managed to cool myself down, I spotted a gentleman who I estimated was in his late sixties standing about 10 feet away from where I was located. For no specific reason I thought to myself, "I hope he doesn't trip on this rowing machine next to me."

Ten seconds later, to my absolute horror, the man lay sprawled at my feet on top of my elliptical, having tripped on the rowing machine next to me!

I am relieved to report that the man did not injure himself and also that due to this incident I found the answer to a question I had asked the Universe about the correlation between *emotion* and *the spoken word* in manifesting an effect around me. At that time though it indeed troubled me to think that I had dragged someone into my weird little world of unfortunate coincidences, but then I thought that there was the possibility that the brief moment this gentleman and I shared could have also been as a result of something he had wished for. The Universe works in mysterious ways.

For the bigger part of my life, much like an untrained superhero, I know I have used this ability to have coincidences happen around me haphazardly and irresponsibly and so it has proven to be both a blessing and a curse. Despite its downside, it has always been fascinating and I have consciously sought out ways to learn more about this phenomenon.

Over the course of the years, I have followed a trail of breadcrumbs and have found pieces of the puzzle in many different places. Journaling and mapping the impossible events that happen around me has also been a key personal practice in uncovering patterns and answers. Understandably, I haven't been too keen in discussing this part of my life with others for when I did so in the past I was met with cynicism, disbelief and deprecation. It wasn't until recent years that the conversation has finally become a trendy topic worthy of book clubs and seminars, much to my enjoyment. But for the most part this has been a lonely journey of self-discovery.

Despite the evidence I had gathered throughout my life, there was a small part of me that wondered if I was making all of this up. It wasn't until 2016 that I finally decided to take ownership of these *impossible coincidences* and get serious about finding answers.

By the year 2017 when I was logging between 5-10 coincidences per day, the word *coincidence* simply did not cut it for me anymore. It just seemed too limiting and hinted at unrelated things that aligned once in a while with no apparent reason, which by then I was certain wasn't the case.

My curiosity was temporarily satisfied when I found the word *synchronicity*, often used to the describe a cluster of 5 or more meaningful coincidences. This word certainly contained more validation for what I was experiencing, but it wasn't until I incorporated the word *postulate* in my vocabulary that I finally started to *crack the code*.

Despite the mayor breakthrough of being able to name what was happening, the bigger questions still remained, *what was I doing and how was I doing it?*

Most of my life I have been a high-performance athlete and movement is a non-negotiable item in my daily schedule and so by 2018 it occurred to me that if I applied the same commitment, I gave to my physical practice to that of my mind I might be able to uncover results faster. It was a no brainer! It was then that I started to dedicate a portion of my day to the practices that resonated the most with me such as meditation, hypnosis and even some of my own invention like meditating with art and movement. The decision to commit to them daily seemed to magnify the synchronicities even more and by the time I was logging close to twenty of them per day it felt like things were getting a little out of hand and so I started to panic.

It was a warm Wednesday night in the middle of the summer and for the first time in 25 years I kneeled down and prayed.

My prayer was specifically directed at Archangel Michael and I conducted it in a conversational tone. I told *my friend* Michael how I was experiencing an insurmountable amount of synchronicities, and although I did not want them to stop, I found myself troubled and unable to manage this level of increased awareness. I asked for his guidance and help in understanding what this meant and for the synchronic events to slow down.

Upon finishing my prayer and just for a brief moment, several pictures from the past flashed in my mind's eye of me as little child walking into my grandmother's bedroom to find her kneeling down and praying. These visions felt sacred and warmed my heart. I thanked Michael for his presence and then I went to sleep.

The next morning around 5:50am both me and my husband were woken up by what I describe as a beautiful music of angelic nature. I heard my husband sigh and then grumble to himself something about how I forgot to disconnect the Bluetooth speakers the night before. He got out of bed and started to make his way downstairs to shut the speakers down. Before he managed to reach the plug, we both heard a man's voice say, "I am here to speak to those who are ready to step into their new selves."

Upstairs, I laid in bed wide awake certain that this message was the answer to last night's prayers. I then thanked "my friend" Michael for the obvious and prompt response.

Following the speaker's event, the synchronicities indeed slowed down and I became more invested in business endeavors. After having worked for one of the largest corporate gyms for 7 years from being a personal trainer and up to the managerial level, I had recently become an independent movement coach and my focus shifted to having clarity on how my gifts would best serve others.

By 2019 I was running a successful and independent business combining two impossible ingredients, art and fitness, and also coaching people in their own journeys of self-discovery. I had grown accustomed to living in a state of awe and now the twenty+ synchronicities a day felt like my daily cup of coffee. In fact they would be triggered upon my command anytime I asked a specific question to the Universe or created a postulate.

I had also grown accustomed to the experience that once in a while the answers did not come wrapped in a gift basket. This was the case when I asked to understand what were the specific ingredients, I needed to have in order to have a postulate manifest within a day.

A couple of weeks after I postulated the question, I was to coordinate and perform a much expected opening act for a fitness organization. On that day one of my cats escaped. This caused a very uncomfortable *feeling in my body* followed by an overwhelming amount of frustration and anguish, after which I heard my *inner voice* say, "Out of all possible days, why did it have to happen today?"

Understandably, my trepidation escalated as I started to think of the dangers in the surrounding area. Knowing better than to continue tumbling down this particular dark hole, I decided to replace this inner dialogue with an image of my cat arriving home safely and I held on to that like a child holding a teddy bear.

After 5 hours of being missing and just 10 minutes before we had to leave the house for the day, my cat Gizmo came back! But by then, I had unleashed a command that would have an impact during the course of my evening performance.

Later that night, I would be the only one in the team to fail at the execution of my own signature move. After having rehearsed it more than a thousand times without ever failing, out of all the possible days to fail, it had to be me on that particular day. And so the words, "out of all possible days, why did it have to happen today?" rang prophetically true for the second time that day.

It wasn't until next morning as I sat sipping my coffee and journaling about these experiences when I realized I had been given the answer to my question of what were the necessary ingredients to have a postulate manifest itself within a day. The escaped cat had triggered the chain of events that led me to find the missing ingredient. I had already figured out that emotions and words put together were part of the recipe, however it became clear to me how experiencing *a physical sensation or feeling in my body* while voicing out my command was the glue that held the spell together. I had read about this in various books and heard it in seminars in the past, but I now understand that actualizing the knowledge through personal experience is also part of the game.

If you are holding this book in your hands and reading these lines, I have also been successful in manifesting a postulate I wrote in one of my journals in 2015. *"The 10 things I need to write a book,"* is written at the top of the page. If you are holding this book in your hands, it also could be as a result of a question you asked or a postulate you created.

It was at the beginning of February of 2020, while driving home from a client meeting where I was pondering upon this realization that I got very excited, squeezed the wheel and yelled, "I think I finally *cracked the code!*" The next day as I got in my car, I noticed there was a crack in the windshield window on the driver's side which had mysteriously appeared overnight. After staring at it for several seconds, I broke out in laughter as I recalled exactly had happened.

Later that week my car dealership called it a *very rare* manufacturing fault. I am happy to report it as a successful postulate.

Please connect with Alejandra Diaz Mercado by email at alediazme@gmail.com

TENACIOUS WOMAN

Marleide Feitosa

My name is Marleide Feitosa and I am originally from Brazil. I've been living in Canada for 25 years.

When I was in grade 7, I was studying about all the countries around the world. My teacher encouraged students to write letters to Consulates or Embassy requesting information about the specific country. I wrote to different Consulates such as Italy, Canada, Finland, Greece, Germany and many other countries. Canada really got my attention because the country has two officially languages English and French. I love to write and I had postulated that one day I will live in country that speaks English and I will improve my communication skills in English and write my books in English and after translate to other languages such as Brazilian Portuguese, Spanish, French, Japanese, Mandarin and many other languages as well. And now many years later I have the opportunity to write my first book in English called *To Daddy With Love*.

This book talks about different kinds of Father Figure. I want my readers to understand that it doesn't matter if they have a father or not, they can choose a male figure to play the role as a father. I talk about Married Father, Step Father, Single Father, Father from the Heart, Future Father, Widowed Father and Addictive Father. I am very proud of myself and very excited about the book because this is my dream from childhood that I always believe that one day I will see my dream come true. The message I want to convey in this book is that unconditional love never fails.

I used to share this dream with friends and people at my workplace. Some they used to laugh and I used to tell them that one day will have my own book written in English and I will invite them to the Launch. Well, well next year on May 01 I will be launching my book and guest what May 01 is also my birthday. I thank my Daddy God, my big brother Jesus, one of my best friend Holy Spirit, family, my daughter Raphaela, grandson Ezra and sons Emmanuel and James-Daniel, Raymond Aaron for offering this amazing 10-10-10 Program that helped me and many other people to get their books out there.

Regarding this book To Daddy With Love by Marleide Feitosa, I am already postulating that it will become New York best seller, I am postulating that it will become a movie, I am postulating that it will be translate in more than 50 languages, I am postulating that before the book launched it will be sold more than 10 thousand copies and also I am postulating that it will help restore many relationship between parents and children and I will include the testimonies on the second edition of this book. I am very excited about the future of this book because I see as my baby that I will give birth and through this book it will help me to make my Perfect Future become reality. My Perfect Future is to become Love's Ambassador on Earth and live my life as a Philanthropist and Humanitarian.

To connect with Marleide Feitosa by email marleidef@yahoo.ca or call her at 647-403-0305

FROM DREAMS TO REALITY

Jen Freilich

It was 2006, I was in my early 30's and a new friend introduced me to transformative power of thought leader and motivational author, Louise Hay, along with Rhonda Byrne, author and creator behind the *The Secret* documentary film. I was immediately drawn to this concept and dove head first down that quantum rabbit hole reading and absorbing everything I could for the next several months.

There was a shift in how I thought, my perspective began to change and I became more focused. I began to realize that my thoughts really do create things and my life on any given day is simply a manifestation of all the thoughts I've previously had. I became very aware of patterns, of events, of signs and other things that showed up in my life. Though, there was a part of me that wondered if it was really that simple, if I could actually manifest the things I wanted or needed in my life. So, I started my first vision board and began to joyfully postulate.

I started to map out my dream life in beautiful photos, inspirational quotes and colorful statements that made it feel as if everything had already come true. Front and center, my main postulate, my first dream home. At the time I felt it had to be realistic enough that I would believe I could actually manifest it within a five-to-ten-mile radius of my family's home.

I started casually looking around, driving up and down streets I thought I might like to live on, in the very neighborhood I thought I wanted to live in, just two miles from my family. I did this for months, casually picking up flyers when I saw a house for sale. To my dismay, all of the homes I was falling in love with started at $600,000. I didn't believe I could manifest that much money, so I decided that my house would cost half that and I believed it would.

My vision board detailed my dream home perfectly, as if I'd already seen a photo of it; light gray with white trim, a burgundy front door, flat usable land, big trees shading the front yard as well as back yard, a white split rail fence around it and one of those giant circular driveways since this is where I planned to expand my established career as a dog trainer with many new guests.

I could already see it clearly in my mind's eye; inside, a spacious and open floor plan, wood floors, fireplace full of personality, office overlooking the training filed, at least three bedrooms, well-lit with natural light through ample windows, so close to the homes of my family members that I could walk there with plenty of land around my home to grow.

With that in mind, I started to allow fear and doubt to creep into my thoughts as my Real Estate Agent drove me to foreclosure after foreclosure. Each of them at the right price, around $325,000. Each of them with potential, but each requiring a minimum of $75,000 for renovations before it was livable, to such a standard that I believed my clients would expect before entrusting me with their canine companions. None of them felt like home.

Something inside me knew I had to take more responsibility for the outcome if I wanted it to be 'my' outcome. I asked my Agent if she would allow me to use her private account to look at listings. My agent also happened to be my client and my friend, I knew she was very busy and thought perhaps this would be helpful for her as well. It was, she agreed and then it happened.

I studied each of the parameters she had entered to see which ones I could manipulate. Something inside me said to lower the property size from 1 acre to 3/4 acre.

There it was. The very first listing. Like magic.

My beautiful home, light gray with white trim. Flat useable land with lush green grass and gorgeous shade trees. In the front yard, a giant Japanese Elm that towers over my home, shading the front during the morning hours. In the back yard, a stunning Mulberry Tree which shades my dog training filed from the afternoon on, gifting us not only with shade to train under all day, but delicious white mulberries as well. Otherwise known as the "treat tree" to the dogs since we can reach up easily and pull off mulberries to reward them for a job well done.

I almost couldn't believe it. The first photo on this listing, nearly identical to the vision I was holding in my mind's eye.

Excitedly, I presented the printed information to my agent while driving to see more foreclosures. While we were looking at other listings, she was actually able to get a hold of the homeowners easily, who just happened to be home bar-b-q'ing and happily invited us over.

This home just happened to be on one of the streets I drove down during the previous months, in the exact neighborhood in which I wanted to live. Walking through the white wrought iron gate for the first time, I see my new avocado tree to the left, and to the right, so many flowers, jasmine growing up the side of the chimney, it's fragrance overwhelming, welcoming me home.

I could feel it. I was walking up to my new front door, which was white, not burgundy as I had on my vision board, but the shutters were burgundy! I took my first steps just inside, looking around I see beautiful real hardwood floors, the original brick fireplace from 1948 in what they had made the dining room, now my cozy living room. To my right, one of the biggest living rooms I had personally seen at that time, so spacious I already knew that would be my personal yoga studio, where I would hold yoga classes, fundraisers, workshops and create an indoor service dog training area.

As I did my first walkthrough the feeling of home grew stronger. The furniture, the candle holders, the picture frames and wall decorations, right down to the paint coloring the walls, was just as if I chose it myself. So much so that as I write this, February 2021, the colors on the walls throughout my home are the exact same, with the exception of only two rooms which begged for a new color.

Walking out the back door, what might be considered a small courtyard is perfect for a couple of kennel runs and now also has a custom aluminum patio cover with lights and ceiling fans for the dogs just in case they should need to spend a couple of hours in there, they will be pampered and comfortable. A lovely and very fruitful lemon tree to my right, so much space in front of me, divided into two very large areas for the dogs to run and play. I head down the extra wide and double extra long driveway, not circular as I postulated, but equally as awesome.

Just ever so slightly above the price range anticipated, reappraisal brought the price of my home down by $10,000. I was still postulating, this is my home, I could feel it, I believed that the rest of the process would be smooth, and with only a couple of small hiccups, everything finally came together nicely. I didn't know it at the time, but I happened to be bidding against my Chiropractor for this property! He's still my Chiropractor and we're still friends.

I moved into my first dream home, which I postulated and manifested, October 2008.

My dream home wasn't the only thing on my vision board between 2006 and 2008. I wanted to fill my new home with love so I set my intentions on finding the love of my life. I thought deeply on this, making a list of qualities and values that a line with mine, the ideal height and age range, profession, lifestyle choices, and so much more. I wasn't really sure if this could actually work, but I was willing to give it a try!

It did. During the same years I met two pretty great guys. I connected with both of them and we became good friends. Both of my new friends matched all of the ideals I had postulated, and though they were very different in many ways, both equally aligned with what I had on my list. They were intelligent and well spoken, we had a lot in common, both were dog trainers, funny, charming, handsome. I thought, this seems too good to be true, but at the very least, I've made two good friends.

As fate would have it, as one year became the next, I grew very close to one of these gentlemen and a relationship blossomed. In the beginning, it was amazing! Better than I could have expected. He was even present at my housewarming party! Things were pretty great for a long time, but they didn't last. At the time I simply couldn't understand what was happening or what went wrong. He became someone I no longer recognized. To be fair, I was barely able to recognize myself. I may never understand what was happening in his life, but I knew the stress of managing a home and business along with an unhealthy relationship was taking its toll on me.

Each week I seemed to feel more and more depressed, my whole body ached, the pain was intense, I felt so sick nearly all of the time. At times I actually felt like I was dying. There was this little voice that began to take over my thoughts. I honestly thought that I had asked for too much, that maybe I didn't deserve so much good, that all of this really was too good to be true.

It would take me a very long time to learn a very valuable lesson when postulating.

The years would pass, the hurt I held so tightly in my heart became unbearable, I couldn't understand what went wrong, but fully understood what it might feel like to die of a broken heart. My body began to deteriorate at a rapid rate, and though I pushed through like a champ for many years, I found myself on medical leave fighting for my life.

July 2018 I was diagnosed with Chronic Persistent Lyme Disease, Babesia, Epstein Barr Virus, Chronic Fatigue Syndrome, Hashimoto's Thyroiditis, Raynaud's Disease, Severe Brain Damage and Mold and Metal Toxicity, to name a few. My body was failing me and time was running out. I didn't have but a few years left in me.

My story was not going to end there.

As I approached the end of my second year on medical leave, having had two years of heavy treatments, terrifying medical episodes, debilitating pain, therapy and countless hours to contemplate life, I decided I needed to live. I was meant to live. I wanted to live.

My parents, who had been trying to get through to me, finally did. I was reminded of all of the wonderful things I had attracted into my life when I was on a completely different wave length, before the damage to my brain from Lyme Disease became severe. I began to look for more answers, I set my intentions to manifest everything I needed to heal and grow and move forward.

The years had beaten me down and my body was vibrating at such a low frequency I found it very difficult to hold positive thoughts or attract the things I needed. Nevertheless, I persisted.

I practiced with little things, easy things. Sometimes it worked and other times it didn't. This was the lesson. As I looked back, I realized that each time I postulated casually, with confidence, as if it already happened, with love and good intentions for the highest good, I vibrated at a higher level and attracted more of the good stuff. When I stressed about it, thought about it all day, believed that something was "too good to be true", let doubt creep in or let fear of having enough "power" to manifest, it backfired.

The second lesson I learned when postulating is, be careful what you ask for. Or don't ask for. I learned that there are a few very key ingredients that shouldn't be missed when trying to attract your kindred spirit. Like, he should also be available. Available emotionally, available to travel, available to enter a new relationship, not currently leaving a relationship. Yes, that part is very important. Timing is everything! Chemistry is important, but missing a few key ingredients and bad timing can interfere heavily. I learned that leaving out something as simple as, *"I am so happy and so grateful that my soul mate also believes I am his soulmate, is free to enter a relationship with me, and is ready for this step in his life."* That would have been helpful for him and me. My postulate in this area is rather casual these days. I simply know when the time is right for both of us, everything will fall into place perfectly, whoever he may be. I whisper to him in the wind knowing that on the right day, he will hear me.

Sometimes the best postulates happen when you least expect it.

Two years ago, while on medical leave at a time when I was not doing so well, I realized one of my service dogs was not getting enough exercise or biological fulfillment. He was becoming increasingly more unhappy, so I determined the best activity we could do together outside of practicing tasks or playing fetch was scent detection. It had been a long time since I had taught scent detection and with the brain damage I was working to heal, needed to find an instructor. I searched high and low, there was no one in my area. I postulated, I put out into the Universe that I needed my ideal instructor to find me. I casually spent time here and there thinking about the qualities that would make this person the ideal instructor for me. Two months later I get an email from a dog trainer, she just moved to this area while under contract for her daytime job as an Immunologist, even doing work with NASA! She only takes on competition clients for Obedience and Scent Detection, she's looking for a place to teach and wonders if I'm interested.

Not only did my newly manifested competition trainer turn both of my service dogs into official AKC show dogs, both excelling in scent detection and obedience, both amassing certifications and new titles, but she played a very real role in helping me heal both physically and mentally. As painful as some of the basic exercises were for me, it got me out of the house, it added more physical activity to my days, it really made me focus and concentrate on so many small details my brain began to heal faster, my muscle coordination began to improve and my strength started to come back. I attracted the perfect competition trainer who knew exactly how to fulfill my dogs and also knew how to help me heal.

Though I had postulate success here and there I was still struggling to hold a positive thought, I wasn't healing as fast as I had hoped, I wasn't able to work more than a few hours a week, I was broke, I had to rebuild my business and it just seemed like my brain was going to be permanently wired for negativity. I needed something. I couldn't even stand myself at times, I was just angry at my situation, blamed the doctors that misdiagnosed me for at least 36 years, angry that I had virtually no help and had negative thoughts about almost everything. I needed a breakthrough, so I sent that postulate out into the universe.

"I am so blessed to have everyone and everything I need to heal already in my life!"

My friend and client, Jacquie Freeman answered. Just as I'm thinking it's time to pull out a few books and create a new vision board, Jacquie sends me a message explaining an incredible opportunity called *The Abundance Experience.* There could not have been a better opportunity than this one and it could not have come at a better time than it did, October 2021.

This experience was out of my budget at the time, but I really wanted to be a part of this. At the time, every dollar I earned went to my medical treatments, medications, supplements, caring for my service dogs and taking care of a household and business. I could feel it, everything about me said, "This is for YOU! Don't miss this opportunity!" I got busy postulating. *"If this is for my highest good, the additional finances will be available in 30 days."* And they were. Those lovely finances that I had asked for arrived just in time and I set out to begin the *The Abundance Experience,* soaking up every word taught to me by the very same mentors I had dreamed of working with from The Secret documentary film, 15 years ago!

This time I didn't allow doubt to enter my mind for one second. I never even thought to udder those dangerous words, "too good to be true."

I said "Thank you!" every day, I gave thanks for the wonderful opportunity I was given, I expressed gratitude to my friend Jacquie Freeman for holding me in her thoughts and including me on this journey. She was about to change my life for the better.

It was time for another vision board. Time to focus on moving forward, healing, growing and postulating. You may be under the impression that creating a vision board is expensive, requires a lot of time, must look fancy, or that you have to spend countless hours in meditation, staring at each item wishing and dreaming it into reality.

I didn't do any of this when I postulated that all of my Amazon packages would be delivered a day early for the month of October. I didn't even write it down. I stated, "I am so happy and grateful now that all of my amazon packages arrive a day early." Then I let it go and forgot I even postulated such a thing. When the next package arrived a day early, I remembered that was a postulate!

If you happen to be a fan of Showtime's Award Winning series *Dexter*, you just might have me to thank for the upcoming revival season. I was fully immersed in this wonderful experience, I listened to every training more than once, took all of the teachings to heart, and felt as if I was starting to vibrate at a higher frequency. As I wrapped up an epic re-watch of the entire series, I said to myself, *"I think it's time for Dexter to come back. I'm not happy with that ending."* I didn't actually intend for it to be a postulate; it was just a single thought. Two days later I'm scrolling on social media and would you know, there was a breaking article stating that *Dexter* is set for revival in 2021 with Micheal C. Hall reprising his role, intending to make good on that ending!

Let me share a secret with you. My vision boards are not fancy or expensive. It's simply a place where I can pin inspiring pictures and write down ideas, thoughts, projects and things I dream of so it's all in one place, right next to my desk. I review it when I have a minute or two, it helps me to stay focused while keeping my eyes on the prize. In fact, I feel like I don't give my vision board nearly enough attention and many postulates that manifest are just quick, single thoughts playfully spoken where only my dogs, Han Solo and Rey, can hear.

The real secret? It's actually not about sitting in front of your vision board all day feeling the feelings of your dreams coming true. It's not even about a vision board, though they can be quite fun to make. I had read and watched "The Secret" documentary a dozen times, but I still didn't fully understand the actual secret. My history demonstrates a pattern of success and lessons when attempting to manifest and I knew I needed a mentor who understood this to the core. I postulated, *"Thank you for making the perfect mentors available to me at the perfect time, in the perfect way, for the perfect monetary exchange."*

It was Raymond Aaron to the rescue!

He came into my life at the perfect time with programs and teachings I was sure he created just for me at this perfect time in my life. He said in regard to responsibility, "It's the willingness to be responsible." Suddenly I could see the light!

When I postulated my home, I was healthier, I was vibrating at a higher level, I was taking responsibility for myself, my actions, my thoughts and working very hard toward my goals. Not just chanting them as affirmations. I was doing my part to make it all happen. I didn't expect The Universe or God to just hand me what I wanted. I put it out there, on my vision board, I drove up and down the streets I wanted to live on in the neighborhood I wanted to live in for several months looking for my home. I would write out new programs, events and activities I would be able to do for my clients when (not if) I lived in my home, right down to how the lessons would be structured and priced.

Placing your postulates on a vision board or even in a notebook is only one possible component, it's not the whole package. Raymond explained, you have to do the work. If you are going to postulate perfect, vibrant health in body, mind and spirit, but you lay on the couch all day eating fast food, you are breaking the laws of the Universe. Your actions do not represent your postulate. You have to be willing to take responsibility by waking up earlier than usual, dedicating yourself to healthy actions like going for a walk, doing a strength workout, meditating, drinking more water and eating healthy organic food.

And this is exactly what I started to do again. Though my illnesses make it terribly painful, beyond uncomfortable and downright impossible at times to wake up early, jump in the shower, eat breakfast and make it to my Zoom meeting with Raymond at 6am (that's a 4am alarm for me), I did it anyway. I asked for it, I postulated, and Raymond provided me with an opportunity of a lifetime and I was not going to let him down or me! I didn't just do it once, I did it for three programs, each three days long, all within two months. If you would have told me back in July 2020, two years after my diagnosis when I only had 5-6 years to live, that by October 2020 I would be working with my dream mentor, getting up at 4am to participate in life changing programs, gaining a publisher and writing not only my first book but also co-authoring a chapter in Raymond Aaron's book and feeling better than I have in many years, I wouldn't have believed you. I wasn't capable of believing anyone at that time. My vibration was too low. I was still in blame mode.

Just 19 days ago from the writing of this chapter February 2021, I was on Zoom with Raymond when he shared how his students were reaching their goals that they thought were unattainable. He asked if there was something that we felt was unattainable in the span of 30 days. I immediately thought to myself, losing 10 pounds in a month is unattainable for me. Perfect vibrant health in 30 days. Make my first million in 30 days. Find the love of my life in 30 days.

Well, as the saying goes, "ask and you shall receive!"

Maybe it should be more like, "get clear about what you want and take responsibility for it and you will receive!"

During this three day workshop I had two of the worst medical episodes that I could remember having in the previous twelve months. One night my body started to go into shock, systems were shutting down, ataxia, my body was having Herxheimer reactions to the die-off of Lyme Spirochetes. I couldn't speak, walk without my service dog by my side or feed myself. With the assistance of my parents, I was able to recover that evening and instead of being fearful or upset that I still had a laundry list of diseases I thanked my body for providing a healing crisis in order to speed up my healing. You see, die-off is good, Herxing means you are killing off the bad stuff and it's looking for a way to exit your body for good. I thanked the Spirochetes for providing valuable lessons in my life, making me an authority on Lyme Disease, being the topic of my first book and giving me the knowledge to help others. I also handed them an eviction notice and asked them to vacate immediately. It's working, I can feel it!

The next night I had the worst Raynaud's flare my cute little toes have ever experienced. They were swollen, bright red, throbbing and so sensitive it literally felt like the tips of my toes were sliced off and the nerve endings were exposed. The slightest touch of even the softest spa socks felt like sandpaper scrapping across nerve endings. I was up most of the night, taking more pain meds and trying to sleep without much luck.

I didn't feel sorry for myself. I wanted to at first. I wanted to fall into, "Why me? Can I just have a break? I can't stand this anymore!" Truth be told, there would be no benefit to that. It wouldn't help me. In fact, the particular set of diseases I have are all invisible. You can't see them unless I point out specific things to you. There is no silver lining like one would think. There is no special treatment, no one feels sorry for you for very long at all. Not with my diseases. In the Lyme community, it's very well known, the exact opposite happens. One by one our friends and family walk away from us. They simply can't understand how sick we are, that we are truly fighting for our lives or why we are still sick years later. It's hard for anyone to wrap their mind around incurable diseases, invisible diseases and lifelong diseases if you don't have one. They can't see my brain damage even if I show them the scan. So when I make verbal mistakes or any mistakes related to the brain damage, they are not forgiven. It generally takes a solid three years and $200,000+ out of pocket to survive the worst part with insurance covering maybe 10%.

I took this opportunity to let all of this go. I recognized that it was no coincidence that I had two of the worst medical episodes in a very long time after postulating perfect, vibrant health. I thanked my body for kicking healing into high gear and I continue to thank my body every day. It's been twenty days since the Raynaud's flare and it is just as bad as it was then. Twenty days of hardly being able to wear shoes and socks or walk, but that doesn't stop me. I believe this is going to be my last Raynaud's flare, ever. I postulated perfect vibrant health and I am getting better every single day in some beautiful way! I am sleeping better, I am finding it much easier to wake up in the morning earlier than usual, I am eating better and I am doing more with my clients and my dogs.

Not only do I feel like I'm vibrating at a much higher, healthier rate, but I've actually had several clients tell me that I look healthier, like I'm glowing! Remember that ten pounds I thought was impossible? I stepped on my scale six days after this program ended, February 4th. I noted my weight in my phone and calculated how much weight I had lost since January 4th: 9.9 pounds!

I might not have made my first million dollars in 30 days, but I did create a powerful shift in my business. Before I became very ill and had to take a medical leave, I had a six-figure business. I knew the business would take a hit while on medical leave since I wasn't able to nurture it, but medical leave rolled right into the pandemic and things went from bad to worse. I missed my clients, I missed meeting new clients, I was very depressed and struggling to gain momentum. I was barely getting a handful of referrals a month and many were not panning out. If this pattern continued, I was going to lose my home. I even had to borrow the money to study with Raymond.

By day two of working with Raymond not only did I get a new client referral, but she signed up for one of the more extensive programs I teach and best of all, she is my ideal client! Our values are completely aligned in all aspects of obedience, health care and nutrition! Just like me, her dog is family. In the 20 days to follow, I have received many referrals, all being my ideal client interested in obedience programs along with guidance in switching their furry family members over to an organic biologically appropriate raw diet. In addition, the Canine Wellness Consulting side of my business has doubled!

I no longer allow myself to doubt or think this is too good to be true. I see everything as a very real possibility, not because of the pixie dust and magic I sprinkle on my vision board, but because I accept the responsibility.

I am willing to accept the responsibility for taking excellent care of myself and healing, for helping others as well as their companion animals heal from Lyme Disease, for telling my story in my own book with the intentions of helping others understand Lyme Disease, prevent it and survive it. I am willing to accept the responsibility for helping many dogs live longer, happier, healthier lives through Canine Wellness Consulting, for helping to bridge the communication gap between humans and animals, for continuing my education on a daily basis, for healing others through my Iyengar Yoga classes, and to help empower women through Belly Dancing.

Will you join me?

Jen Freilich is an Owner, Trainer, and Behavior Specialist, for more information please go to www.attheendofyourleash.com

IS IT A MIRACLE OR
IS IT A POSTULATE?

Christine Green

My Postulate story starts when I was sixteen years old. I didn't know what a postulate was then, or that it would have such a far-reaching effect on me so many years later, but it did. Allow me to explain. At sixteen I was a receptive child, I lived in Kenya and I met a teacher who took me on one side and told me the following: "Think of it like this—you're a cell in the mind of the Universe and this means that you can communicate with anyone, anywhere, whether or not you already know them."

At the time I was fascinated with what he had to say. I felt privileged that he had chosen to give me this information and, although I didn't know what to do with it then, I retained it and thought about it a lot.

When I was 25, I went to California. I lived in Marin County and sometimes visited San Francisco. On one of my trips to San Francisco, I lost my purse. It contained my Social Security card which gave me a right to be in America, and it contained more money than I could afford to lose—I was just a nanny at the time, earning very little.

On that trip to America, I was inspired. I channeled poetry, spiritual poetry, and it poured out of me like water from a tap. These poems were deep and meaningful, and I felt privileged to have them flow through me in the way that they did. It happened after a psychic chose to paint a painting for me. I never asked for the painting, but it was the most beautiful thing that I'd ever seen.

At the time that I received the painting, I also received a cassette recording. On this recording I was told that four days before I listened to the cassette I would have begun to write and that the writing would change my life. Again, I felt incredibly privileged. I couldn't quite get my mind around the fact that I'd been singled out in this way, nor that someone who knew nothing about me could predict that I would have started something that I'd never done before and be right about my activity's days earlier. I thought the words I channeled must be very important so, as each poem came, line by line I learned them off by heart. I can still remember them today.

When I found myself in San Francisco with no purse, those two postulates came together in my mind and worked as a team. One was the words the teacher who had impressed me at sixteen had said and the other was one of my poems, and these two postulates made a miracle happen that day.

I barely had time to think intellectually about the situation. When I realised that the purse was missing and that it contained a document that I could ill afford to lose, my stomach began to do belly-flops as I registered the full implications. I knew instantly, without even thinking, that I needed to broadcast a message to the Universal Mind, powerfully and fast. The words of one of my poems flooded my mind and two lines kept repeating over and over again: 'I learned to ask for what I needed; On my hands and knees I got down and pleaded; Then I learnt to thank, and that's the key to Heaven's bank!'

It never entered my head to worry about what people might think—I just knew that to connect with the Universal Mind I needed to use emotion. I hollered. I screamed. I shrieked and I shouted. My body shook. I fully expressed the full magnitude of my distress. Unsurprisingly, somebody asked me what the matter was! She said she'd never seen anyone so distressed. I explained and she gave me a dollar to pay for the bus home.

Once I was on the bus the words of my poem repeated over and over again: 'Then I learned to thank, and that's the key to Heaven's bank'. I had a portable cassette recorder with me and headphones. I also had a recording of myself singing hymns, childhood hymns of Praise, and I had a recording of myself singing my own spiritual songs.

I put on the headphones and, in my mind, I sang with all my heart. I figured that the most powerful part of my mind was the primitive child inside. I've never in all my life sung with such joy and such meaning. The journey took an hour and by the time I arrived home I was in a seriously uplifted state of mind and being. Five minutes after I got in, the doorbell rang. A complete stranger with a big smile on his face stood in the doorway and these were his words, „I don't know what made me drive half an hour out of my way to bring you your purse but here it is!"

I was speechless with joy, dumbfounded for a moment and I could barely believe how lucky I'd been, how treasured by the Universal Mind. I asked, "How did you know where to bring it to me?" He replied, "I looked inside your purse and a little while ago you cut out an article from a newspaper. You filled in your address in order to receive the words of a prayer for abundance. You never sent it, so your address was in your purse." I thanked him profusely again and he went on his way. I went back indoors and spent a long time thinking about the magical elements which made that situation occur.

Had I known the meaning of the word 'postulate' I would have been able to see how lucky I was to have all the ingredients in my mind with which to make a miracle. I've gone on from that day with the postulate 'I am part of the whole' ringing in my heart. That helpful, powerful way of thinking has given me a charmed and magical life in which I've helped many people to help themselves, and in which I've had many, many moments of pure joy.

I'm the author of 'The Book on Hypnotherapy: Facts and True Life Stories to Show You How and Why It Can Work for You' and I'm a teacher of hypnotherapy. I love to give people tools which can make a real difference to their lives. People come on my courses for two reasons—one is that they want a new career, the second is that they want self-mastery and they want the tools to take their own mind in hand and so make miracles for themselves.

I also teach Reiki and self-awareness. When I teach Reiki this way, I use diagrams to help people access a deeper part of their mind and being. Many people have told me that these diagrams have changed their lives. This is because they're subjective and they help you to see your blind spots and understand how your subconscious mind is affecting you. They help you to have more understanding for yourself and for others, and they teach you what will and won't change in others' behaviour. Because they're diagrams and you're looking at them, you can have a chance to look at things that you don't want pointed out to you, but in your own time and in your own way. I firmly believe that you need access to what you don't know is causing a problem before you can fix it.

What people have often said about me is, 'Christine, you're more than a hypnotherapist, you're more than a Reiki teacher, you're more than a practitioner—you're unstoppable, you won't give up and you always find a way.'

I've been called an Angel, a Guardian Angel, a Fairy Godmother, a magician, a shepherd and a miracle worker. People say that they couldn't have done it without me. This is because I have such a comprehensive understanding of the mind, the subconscious mind and of people's emotions and people's behaviour. It's also because if people want to change their behaviour, I can help them do it, and because if they need someone to depend on while they make changes, my shoulders are broad, and they can depend on me—I *will* come through for them.

I've helped 70-year-old agoraphobics who've been that way all their lives travel to a foreign country; people who were about to sabotage their relationships to stop their self-destructive behaviour; people to save their marriage and people who really needed to split up to do so with kindness and understanding; I've helped people who have no backbone to get one; I've helped children, I've helped sports people and business people to excel; I've helped people to lose weight and people to become kinder. Whatever *you* want from *you*, I can help you to get it—because I absolutely believe you have it in you, and I *will* bring out the best in you.

Information on upcoming courses and classes with Christine Green, please go to one of these websites: www.advancedhypnosis4u.com, www.bookonhypnotherapy.com, www.reiki-healing-basingstoke. co.uk. Christine's direct email address is christine@advanced hypnosis4u.com

FEEL THE YEARN:
HOW TO LOVE YOUR POSTULATES

Lisa Honeywell

A few weeks after returning to my home in the US, the world as we knew had significantly changed. Thanks to my persuasive inner voice, I scheduled my trip precisely when I did, another opportunity would not have presented itself for many months to come, as travel came a screeching halt with the global lockdown.

What's extraordinary about this timeline is that the documentary movie that I filmed the previous month, was in editing to be released to a worldwide captive, on demand audience. I didn't know anything about film speed, geogating, closed captioning or partnering with a world renown video streaming platform. I literally awoke at 4AM one morning with a burning desire to film a documentary. How? I had no idea how, that didn't matter, I was on a mission with the intention to achieve my new postulate. That's right, I produced and launched my doc in less than three months at the inception of a lockdown.

Loving what you do is the single most important life hack to attaining your postulates. It's my opinion, that when you love what you do and do what you love, the chances are extremely high that you will LOVE the postulates that you create as well. To enhance your success, you've got to feel the yearn!

Imagine a powerful key that activates your postulates, welcoming them into your reality. The key is energetic in nature rather than in physical form. Rivers of intentions flow through your mind, allowing this energetic key to gently unlock any uncertainties about your postulates manifesting. Without certainty, you would have a murky soup of doubt and counter postulates requiring you to perform a detox cleanse to rid less -than-optimal thoughts. Have a clear and worthy postulate, access love to set your intention and uplevel your outcome with unwavering enthusiasm and focused determination. Now is the time to flex your creative neurons!

As a youth, I selected a book from our family library. After completion, I immediately began to practice the concepts. Application is a basic component to the magical recipe. Giving your brain a whirl with new ideas, logic and universal laws may strengthen your neural pathways however without actual application, you've only redeemed a good mental workout. Practicing the techniques is a game changer. Endless possibilities for personal enhancement exist.

The first step that I learned was to target a particular outcome that I wished to achieve. The next step was to imagine that my desired outcome had already been accomplished. This worked so well that I wondered, if I'd jumped a dimension, managed to portal to distant future, experienced remote viewing of my upcoming future or if I had taken a deep dive into my mind creating my own new reality.

The truth is that we all practice these techniques daily consciously or unconsciously. That's right! You get what you think about and focus your attention on most of the time, whether you are aware of it or not. Allow time each day for your self-reflection and meditation, being mindful of the quality of your thoughts.

The next step was to imagine the way that I felt in my dream come true scenario on a physical, mental and emotional level. I readily embraced this idea checking in with myself frequently capturing my true feelings during my visualizations.

On one occasion, I imagined that my name was announced over the microphone as the winner of a prestigious competition. I visualized the intricately ornate details of my stage ensemble, the feeling of joy radiating in my heart as I stood before the cheering audience. I practiced this technique often enough, that on the day of the actual event, I gave my presentation and received my award exactly as I had envisioned. There were no surprises, at least not for me. This scene had played out so many times in my mind's eye that I knew in which direction I would look when receiving the prizes and precisely how I would feel.

My mental dress rehearsals consisted of intense focus of my desired outcome and the corresponding feeling elicited from the imagery. I was convinced that practicing these techniques proved to be highly effective and productive.

Early on, I became apprehensive and temporarily refrained from practicing my visualizations in competitions. Having won so many contests, I elected instead to allow others the lovely opportunity to experience a good win. Today I encourage anyone willing to apply themselves wholeheartedly to use these techniques to reap the benefits of optimal health, happiness, and success.

Receiving excellent coaching and continued study, I upped my game implementing three additional techniques; directing my attention to the postulate for a specific length of time (duration) of focused intention, the number of times throughout the day (frequency) that I visualized my desired outcome and lastly, the distraction free (intensity) that I projected my desired intention.

WOW! Everything showed up even quicker than I had ever imagined. Two weeks after incorporating the three additions learned in my training, I purchased a new black luxury car. What's interesting and a bit humorous about this situation is that I already owned a beautiful luxury car that I adored driving, however as I listened to the audios on the power of thought, the example that was repeatedly given throughout the lectures was a specific type of black luxury car that I now found myself driving. Seriously it all happened in two weeks.

Shortly thereafter, I attended a conference and during the book signing I thanked the author of the book and audiobook profusely for the sharing his "uncut" version of these techniques. While on stage with him, I mentioned my new car acquisition, adding that upon arrival at LAX, my car rental had been magically upgraded at no additional fee to a maxed-out luxury vehicle for my ten day stay on the west coast. I credited the author for his masterful teaching techniques which I used to create my lovely reality.

Incredible outcomes defying time, distance and all logic continue to show up for me. All concerns of the "how" simply melt away when practicing these techniques, I keep my focus on my postulate.

Whenever I am asked if it's necessary to perform all of the steps that I've mentioned above? My reply is ...no, it's not. There have been times that I have glanced at something beautiful for a brief moment, and only once at that, however with intense admiration and love, never thinking about it again (consciously at least) to find myself later admiring that exact piece of art in my living room. That's when the realization usually hits me .... I notice that I've had an intense appreciation for something, as brief as it may have been and thought to myself, I would absolutely love that, while experiencing simultaneous joy.

I have immense gratitude for all of the authors, presenters and educators who have shared their knowledge and universal secrets so that others may successfully navigate and prosper here on planet Earth. Presently I have an incredible mentor, I continue to read tons of books and consistently participate in opportunities to upgrade and optimize my performance.

There is no limit (unless self-imposed) to use these techniques. Keep excellent company to elevate your spirit and thoughts. Protect your mind. Take a good look and consider the following Q C questions. What do you listen to? Who do you listen do? What do you watch? Who are your friends? Yes, it's about quality control and you're the one in charge.

QC is much like gardening, flowers, shrubs, and trees are pruned to help produce more flowers and fruit. Pesky weeds may be extracted from the landscape as well. Your brain engages in its own synaptic pruning. Neuroplasticity is your friend. Remove what no longer works for you and strengthen what does.

Consuming supplements is less effective when your body is exposed to junk. I've trained with a human potential leader who refer to the bad stuff as kryptonite. Junk drains your body, mental clarity and emotional fortitude, consequently the supplements you've ingested will be of little value. Remove the kryptonite first; low vitality food, excitotoxins, alcohol, drugs, contaminants in topical skincare and dental products, environmental and food mold and of course people. Pull the weeds so that your garden may flourish.

Movement is essential, walk, dance, stretch, strive for direct sun on your skin daily. If that's not possible, incorporate quality lighting in your home and office. Learn a new language or instrument, develop something in a field different from your own or design or patent something to enrich the overall health of the planet.

Honestly, why spend your valuable time focusing on noteworthy goals or postulates if your mind is cloudy with toxins and your body is full of garbage? Once you begin to minimize and eventually eliminate the toxins, you will notice that your strength rapidly increases magnifying your reach and ability to project more powerful outcomes. Your postulates will show up quicker with greater ease. Be clean and think clean!

One of my postulates was to author a few books. I attended a workshop in Canada arriving the night before the event. The next morning, before sunrise, I eagerly ran out into the snow massaging icy crystals all over my face while treading a path around the hotel grounds. According to the local newspaper it was coldest day on record at that point in the year. I absolutely hit the postulate jackpot on this one. The previous day I anticipated the rejuvenating effects soon to be mine in the extreme cold awaiting me. Back in Texas our average temperature was 100 degrees with high humidity. I postulated on one sweltering day that I would be in extreme cold before I knew anything about this workshop. The uplifting, invigorating air made me feel as though I had become... "one with the universe." I've experienced similar feelings on my trips to Iceland, super charged and in awe of mother nature's incredible diversity. Could be that that specific geographical areas offer energetic benefits as well?

Entering the hotel, I continued my morning run meandering through the corridors intentionally skipping past the equipment available in the gym enclosure. When I noticed a ping-pong table in the atrium near the pool, my postulate instantly presented itself. I would play a competitive game during my stay. I haven't played many games; however, I was in the market shopping for a ping-pong table and was eager to begin this new activity. Mid-day, I walked past the table at the exact same time as another workshop attendee, striking up a conversation with her, asking if she would be interested in a game. What are the chances that she had been the ping-pong champion at her school in Egypt? Game on, she politely kicked my butt as I reveled in the majesty and incredible wow factor over the synchronicity of events that led us to the table at that precise moment in time.

During the day I postulated the perfect meal that I would enjoy that evening for dinner. That night as I studied the menu displayed on the easel at the entrance to the restaurant, the maître d came out to greet me. I explained to him that what I desired, a petite portion of wild rice and steamed vegetables was nowhere on the menu. He said, "one moment, let me see what I can do" spun around and disappeared. No sooner than he walked away, he magically reappeared with a glorious tray heaping with mounds of wild rice and vegetables. I presented my credit card and he replied, "it's on the house" and then disappeared. Wow, that worked out well, even better than I anticipated.

The following day I was invited to lunch by the presenter. Sure, my postulate was to absorb as much information from this brilliant titan of industry as possible however my own expectations were blown! I experienced a one-on-one conversation with him that wasn't on my radar. I learned what a kind and caring soul he truly is, striving to give his students the exact tools that they need to succeed, and I was treated to lunch! Triple Wow!

One evening after the workshop, our group met for dinner at an elegant restaurant not far from the hotel. I postulated that I would ride to dinner with someone that I'd enjoy knowing. The lady who offered me a lift was an absolute dear, we discovered that we both were trained in a particular science and technology. This was a unique opportunity for a meaningful communication exchange. Wow!

On the last day of my workshop, there was a drawing with a variety of exciting prizes to be awarded to attendees. The grand prize winner would receive a ticket to a spectacular VIP event with highly acclaimed speakers and a choice of venues in either the US or Canada. I wanted the grand prize and knew that it was meant for me. I envisioned myself seated in the VIP section, having the highly touted special photo opportunity with presenters. Before the winner's name was called, I angled my chair clearing enough space to allow me to sprint to the front of the room to claim my prize. I was sitting in the front row, a somewhat nerdy thing that I tend to do, however I didn't want to stand up too soon, it would appear awkward, I had to wait until I actually heard my name. Finally, my name was called, I jumped up dancing with glee to accept my prize. Wowwegazowee!

Although many of the examples that I've provided may seem somewhat ordinary, I assure you that I have also realized some of the most outrageous feats of extraordinary occurrences imaginable. I intend to elaborate in detail in the near future.

Lisa Honeywell is the award-winning author of the upcoming book, *Make Money Being Watched, How To Get Paid Residually Making Movies*. Lisa's organizational roadmap with time saving hacks is certain to inspire up and coming short and documentary filmmakers.

For more information on Lisa Honeywell, please go to MakeMoneyBeingWatched.com

FULL SCHOLARSHIP

Olga Kaminer

I was 24 years old, a single mom with a 1-year-old child, just completed my BSc degree in Industrial Engineering and got accepted into the Masters program at Technion, Israeli Institute of Technology, a very elite university. My postulate was to get a full scholarship to complete my Masters. Full scholarship meant that my tuition would be paid for, I will get monthly scholarship money on top of that and will be allowed to serve as a teaching assistant at the maximum capacity allowed.

The decision whether or not to award scholarship always came after the letter of acceptance to the program came in.

That day I went to the Dean's office and he told me that I was a very bright student. However, he was very sorry to inform me that all full scholarships have been already taken. He offered me a partial scholarship. I replied that I deserved the full scholarship, I worked very hard to get it and I won't get a NO for an answer. After some time that day, while I was still in his office, his assistant entered the room and said that a certain student decided to drop the graduate program and won't be coming back. That meant that a full scholarship just became available. At this moment, the Dean looked at me and said "wow, you are so lucky, the scholarship is yours".

My postulate came true! And the Universe started working on my postulate way before I came to meet with the Dean, because that student had to come to the decision to drop the program.

Olga is now a College Professor, Pure-Life Coach, Author, and Speaker. To connect with Olga, go to www.olgakaminer.com.

A LESSON IN TRUST: DOES TRUE LOVE REALLY EXIST?

Amy Lemire

Does true love really exist? I considered this question in January of 2019 and I felt empty and confused. Maybe true love is only for the few and those lucky enough to find it and experience it. The year started off in with my divorce being final, at the end of January. Let me clarify, it not just a divorce, it was the second divorce in my life. I felt disillusioned and began to think that maybe I was meant to be single the rest of my life. In June, I decided to attend a self-development workshop, Life Mastery, looking at 2019 as my year of a transition to life at a new level. I began to wish secretly that one day, I would find true love and meet the man of my dreams.

At the event I was attending in June 2019 there was an evening all about relationships. The facilitator instructed us that people in relationships would fill out one page in their workbook, but people like me, not in a relationship, would fill out a different page. He explained that we all had either happiness when it came to relationships or we may have some serious pain from the past, but either way, we needed to come into this part of the workshop with a very open mind of creation. He persuaded us to stay and not leave and I listened. I recall for a split second feeling curious as I began to write in my workbook. After many months of anger and resentment about the failed relationships with men in my life, I was no longer angry or upset that my second marriage had ended in divorce. I was not sad about being alone again at a later stage of my life, I was not jealous or resentful of all the people around me who had the perfect relationship that I did not have in my life. I chose to focus on curiosity thoughts, to engage in the exercise with a positive and open mind.

The exercise was to list everything that I wanted in my relationship. I had done this activity in the past, painting a vision of the perfect partner—but the second step is what made it different for me this time. The second step of the exercise was to list out what I would NO LONGER tolerate in my relationships with men. I thought 'what are my boundaries?' for the first time in my life. This opened the door for me. I allowed myself to see and it was a huge breakthrough. I began to realize that many of my relationships with men in my life entailed taking care of someone, feeling like I always needed to fix somebody, rescue them, to the point where it was codependent and I always ended up feeling empty, used, and in both marriages financially tapped out. My thought habits in relationships had no focus on my personal boundaries. I felt a sense of power and confidence as I got very clear about what I would no longer tolerate in my intimate relationships anymore. The theme for 2019 became to raise my standards in my life, and most importantly boundaries in my relationships with men.

Fast forward to August 2019. I was grateful that I had decided back in 2018 to sign up for Raymond's transformational retreat in Cancun. I decided the second day of the workshop to end a dating relationship because the person was not meeting the standards I had set for relationships. As I shared this with the class,

I remember feeling vulnerable wondering if people would see me as being weak or judge me—but I stood strong in my decision. I felt a new inspired power, as I had decided I was worth more. It was my birthday week and I was excited to celebrate a new year, said loudly with enthusiasm!

One of my friends asked me to come to a restaurant for dinner the night before my birthday, August 27, 2019. I was excited about the many new friends I had already made at the retreat and was ready for a fun night, starting a new chapter of my life. Halfway through the dinner, with two full tables of people, Nigel, a charming man from the UK, made a suggestion that we all switch tables before dessert. When he came to me to ask me to switch tables I felt this energizing spark. There was something there between us, a feeling that I'll never forget. I went and sat by him. As we began to talk, the birthday cake came out and everyone sang Happy Birthday to me (in several different languages). It was the best birthday I have ever had. Later that night, we all went dancing and Nigel told me 'We British men treat women different than American men.' I said, 'you will have to show me how.' That was the moment he captured my heart and my true love appeared in my life. I later found out in the evening that he was the instigator of the whole night. We spent much time together that week getting to know each other and talking and sharing some of the challenges in life and relationships we had both experienced. We had so much in common.

It is now February 2020. I'm happy to say that I have found my true love. I am so inspired not only by Nigel but by my decision to focus on my 'relationship boundaries' and my 'healthy thought habits,' that I became a Peak Performance Thought Habit Coach, helping others to identify if their though habits are supporting or sabotaging their success. I want to give the power of postulating to others. My thought habits helped me find the love I dreamed about at the workshop in June 2019. This is the first time in my life I have felt I am in a love partnership, with a best friend. My love Nigel is someone who makes me want to be more than I am today. He inspires me and is devoted to me. He is a partner that keeps me grounded when the world seems to be falling down. He makes me laugh and smile. Nigel is a true romantic. A man who completes me and teaches me. Someone that has high standards and makes me raise my standards. Most importantly, a soulmate who is the source of a love that is so beautiful and powerful that I know it is one thing—true love.

Amy Lemire is a Peak Performance Habit Coach, please connect with her by email amy@aimwithamy.com or phone 847-531-3561. For additional information please go to www.aimwithamy.com

DOUBLEBLESSED.COM

Douglas Mercer

This writing is dedicated to my ancestry, great-grandparents, grandparents, parents, siblings, nieces, nephews, great-nieces, great-nephews, aunts, uncles, cousins, and relatives. Furthermore, a particular thanks of gratitude goes to my mentor Raymond Aaron (my publisher, mentor, and teacher) and his excellent and talented staff. Many thanks go to my Reverend Dr. Terry Cole-Whitaker; Maryanne Williamson; Bob Proctor; Marci Shimoff; Dr. John Gray, Ph.D.; Dr. Master Sha, MD, LPH, and his research team Dr. Peter Hudoba, MD, and Dr. Genvieve Julian, PhD.; Dr. Arvind Baliga MD; Joe Williams, MA, LPC, LCADC; Doug Reichert, MA, LPC; Barbara Sorace, MSW, LCSW, LCADC; John McLernon, MSW, LCSW; Ed Kyle, EEO Chief; my Success Principles Coach Jack Canfield; My Morning Mentor Mary Morrissey; Ken Wilber; Robert Widitz, BS; Patricia Diamond, Head of Human Services Atlantic County, NJ; Ben Mount, Division Director of Public Health of Atlantic County; Jerry DelRosso, Atlantic County Administrator: and Dennis Levinson, County Executive for Atlantic County. A perpetual heartfelt thanks to my life-long childhood friends, ex-wife, ex-fiancée, ex-girlfriends, past lovers, long time friends, new and close friends, recovery community and sponsors, coaches and mentors, educators, colleagues, leadership, teachers and instructors, scholar-practitioner classmates, students, clients, spirit guides, counselors, and treatment providers, and the souls I meet along the road to happy destiny. If it were not for God, I do not know what my life would be like. I thank you, God, the Divine.

> "T-1.I.2. Miracles as such do not matter. The only thing that matters is their Source, which is far beyond evaluation" (A Course in Miracles, p. 84, Foundation for Inner Peace).

We are ultimately One.

"Nothing real can be threatened"
(A Course in Miracles, p. 83, Foundation for Inner Peace).

In 2005 I was in a multi-car accident that resulted in a broken back but did not break me nor my spirit. No one else was hurt. I believe that my prayers for others to be safe were answered. I didn't include me. My postulate (prayer) was "Don't let anyone get hurt," as I was thinking about others that were in the van (10 passengers). My passengers were saved from injury, but I was not included at that moment. My postulate came true for everyone else; had I postulated like a pro, I probably would not have been hurt too. Several vehicles were involved: the car that had run the stop sign and hit us on the right side, pushing my vehicle into the oncoming lane and the oncoming traffic resulting in a subsequent strike to the van and head-on into a tree the other side of the highway. The cars that were traveling along with the flow of traffic hit the vehicle that had hit us. How no one else in the multi-car accident did not get hurt at all is truly a mystery. I believe that my prayers were effective is all I can say about it. I was immediately transitioned into a time warp of slow-motion experience that allowed me to experience the whole accident in detail and think through to draw all danger emotionally-energetically to me, so much so that the focal point was directed to my spine and snapped my back. I knew that if

I were to get out and stand up, that nerve damage would have been more complicated than it was. I asked everyone in the van if they were okay, and to my relief, they were fine, a bit shaken up but okay. I thanked God for answering my prayers for their well-being. The journey took me to three hospitals and a long journey back to 30% disability. If it weren't for the tremendous medical attention received and alternative healing modalities, I might not be walking on my own today.

"Nothing unreal exists"
(A Course in Miracles, p. 83, Foundation for Inner Peace).

They say that everything that occurs in life is a blessing, and to some degree, it was. The nine months out of work on disability and under that wonderful care of my mother, relatives, friends, and medical team of doctors, nurses, and ancillary support. My bosses, Harry Morgan, and Dave Woolbert, my chiropractor, and my girlfriend gave me self-help materials and nutritional information. My mother, whom I love and hold great esteem, had alternative suggestions to allopathic medicine along with motherly advice and love for me. My mother flew out to New Jersey to be with me by my hospital bedside and brought me back to Oracle, Arizona, for follow-up physical therapy and physical recovery. My aunts Mary and Dana invited me to stay with them for a while during the recuperation period. Joe Williams (my good friend and boss) had visited me in Phoenix, AZ. During my second hospital, where the surgery took place, the nursing staff told my mother that they had never had a patient who received as many visitors I had and wanted to know if I was famous (aha). Famous, no, just a person who was appreciated, loved and received so much kindness from many friends that visited throughout the hospital stay for my back surgery. By the end of the week, there were so many of my friends, clients, and coworkers that the hospital staff wheeled me down to the lobby full of caring people poring out loving energy.

It was miraculous. "T-1.I.3. Miracles occur naturally as expressions of love. The real miracle is the love that inspires them. In this sense everything that comes from love is a miracle" (A Course in Miracles, p.83, Foundation for Inner Peace).

"Herein lies the peace of God"
(A Course in Miracles, p. 83, Foundation for Inner Peace).

My spirit was lifted that carried me through and for the many years thereafter, reflecting on all the love that was poured out for my wellbeing and recovery from back surgery. My ex-wife Shireen reached out to me and gave prayers of support; she is very spiritually blessed.

I got in touch with the Power of Now by Tolle and Primal Diet through my dear friend Dr. Theresa McReynolds, DC. I studied Clayton College (closed), where I was going for a Ph.D. in Naturopathic methods aligned with my mother's philosophy in natural healing principles. "T-1.I.4. All miracles mean life, and God is the Giver of life. His Voice will direct you very specifically. You will be told all you need to know" (A Course in Miracles, p. 84, Foundation for Inner Peace).

"T-1.I.5. Miracles are habits, and should be involuntary. They should not be under conscious control. Consciously selected miracles can be misguided" (A Course in Miracles, p. 84, Foundation for Inner Peace).

Another story further into my past was a pastor who informed me of a spiritual trying to get my attention from years ago. In essence, I told her that I was not going to pursue her idea. But she insisted that I pay attention to the message. She informed me that she was an empath, and I am too, but I didn't know it at the time. Okay, I said to her (to appease her). Okay, then, prove it. How? We agreed on a sign. I said, if a blue feather appears within one week, I'll accept that as a noticeable sign. I derived the thought of a blue feather from the cover of a favorite book, Illusions: A Reluctant Messiah by Richard Bach.

She said, that's great, it will happen. She seemed confident that a blue feather would appear for me without a doubt. Skeptical, I went about my business.

That was a Sunday. By the very next Sunday, I walked into a concluding service conference of about 100 participants in Boston, Massachusetts, along with my friend Ethelyn Randall—lo & behold, there it was, my sign! Baskets of feathers on each conference table.

The baskets were filled with various colors of feathers...two versions of blue feathers, light and dark blue! The baskets of feathers had a rainbow variety of colors, but two versions of blue were the only colors that were doubled. Now, if that was not a clear sign of the divine getting in touch with me, then call it coincidence. Carl Jung would have plenty to say about coincidences.

There was a bit, my sign on Sunday exactly the following weekend. (a spirit guide was trying to get a hold of me since TCW ministries in 1979, according to my lover, Eileen).

"T-1.I.6. Miracles are natural. When they do not occur something has gone wrong" (A Course in Miracles, p. 84, Foundation for Inner Peace).

My Second Recovery from Active Alcoholism

"T-1.I.7. Miracles are everyone's right, but purification is necessary first" (A Course in Miracles, p. 84, Foundation for Inner Peace). Another story for the postulates: the spirit had been kicked out of me from 1981-1982 to homelessness. After five years of sobriety, I had a relapse back into alcoholism. Unbeknownst to me, I had drifted from a conscious connection from God. Not only was I back to getting drunk, but without a spiritual connection and did not know until re-entry into treatment. While homeless, I ended up staying in shelters for the homeless and sought to get on Antabuse (a deterrent medication to drinking). Upon inquiry, a social worker referred me to the hospital to get a prescription for the medication (an aversive medication-assisted treatment). Where I arrived, it was not an Antabuse clinic; it was a hospital rehab for alcoholics (there was no such thing as an Antabuse clinic). The Alcohol Evaluation and Treatment Center (AETC) a unit at the hospital, admitted me for inpatient treatment.

While there, I had an awakening halfway through the course of treatment. I was having trouble with the AA message and reference to God. My ears hurt to hear anyone say, God. Then, during a meeting, a little willingness appeared about my beingness. That night, I had prayerfully requested to be restored to sobriety... (long story short) I have been sober ever since 1982. Thanks be to God and messengers along the way! "T-1.I.8. Miracles are healing because they supply a lack; they are performed by those who temporarily have more for those who temporarily have less" (A Course in Miracles, p. 84-85, Foundation for Inner Peace).

My First Recovery from Active Alcoholism

"T-1.I.9. Miracles are a kind of exchange. Like all expressions of love, which are always miraculous in the true sense, the exchange reverses the physical laws. They bring more love both to the giver and the receiver" (A Course in Miracles, p. 85, Foundation for Inner Peace).

My father introduced me to my first AA meeting when I was turning 19. My brother and childhood friends can tell you that I was a falling-down drunk. I was embarrassed and felt ashamed that I could not stay sober and, in the end, became a wino drunk on the park bench in Tucson, AZ. "T-1.I.10. The use of miracles as spectacles to induce belief is a misunderstanding of their purpose" (A Course in Miracles, p. 85, Foundation for Inner Peace.). I did the geographical cures that never worked and ended up in treatment twice at 19 years old. The treatment program Director, Dr. Ken Swift, informed me that the program took me in before age eligibility of 20 years and older. From there, I sobered up and remained so for five years. My prayers were answered. "T-1.I.11. Prayer is the medium of miracles. It is a means of communication of the created with the Creator. Through prayer love is received, and through miracles love is expressed" (A Course in Miracles, p. 85, Foundation for Inner Peace). My drunken experiences got me kicked out of Warner Erhard's forum spinoff est workshops. Showing up drunk to a self-improvement program does not work well. Booze and getting well is a bit of cognitive dissonance.

First Annual Alcoholics Olympics

"T-1.I.12. Miracles are thoughts. Thoughts can represent the lower or bodily level of experience, or the higher or spiritual level of experience. One makes the physical, and the other creates the spiritual" (A Course in Miracles, p. 85, Foundation for Inner Peace). I was a year sober and getting healthy, and along came the opportunity to enter the First Annual Alcoholics Olympics. I joined the track team, tried out, trained, and performed. It turned out I was put on the last of a four-member relay team. It turns out, the last member of the team is counted on to make up for lost time if behind. To get the concept, watch the movie, Drunk Parents. As it turned out, we won first place for the relay team, and I won first place for the 50-yard dash. An angry fellow got into my face as

I hold the two metals and told me that he would be holding those metals if he were to have showed up on time. He who hesitates is lost. The universe likes speed, showing up, and taking action.

Step Work in Recovery Continued

"T-1.I.13. Miracles are both beginnings and endings, and so they alter the temporal order. They are always affirmations of rebirth, which seem to go back but really go forward. They undo the past in the present, and thus release the future" (A Course in Miracles, p. 85). To stay sober, do the program for recovery. The miracle of recovery principles is that healing nature transmutes the past shame and guilt into strengths covered out of character weaknesses. The Pleasure Unwoven by Dr. Kevin McCauley explains it as not all brains are created equal. There are tough and resilient brains that do not succumb to the adverse effects of alcohol. Others may have a genetic predisposition or vulnerability to the effects of alcohol, and I fell on the latter occasion. The changes in the brain of an alcoholic are reactive to the alcohol and change more quickly to become addicted than most brains. That is a good thing that most people do not have to worry about drinking too much and becoming dependent.

However, a brain that is malleable to alcohol can also rebound in recovery. Nature favors adaptability, and a malleable brain is flexible, and flexibility can become an asset in recovery. Recovery can be passed on is the good part of the story, and we do not always hear about that. We mostly listen to lectures about passing on the genetics of the disease. "T-1.I.14. Miracles bear witness to truth. They are convincing because they arise from conviction. Without conviction they deteriorate into magic, which is mindless and therefore destructive; or rather, the uncreative use of mind" (A Course in Miracles, p. 85).

Meeting Rev Dr. Terry Cole-Whitaker

T-1.I.15. Each day should be devoted to miracles. The purpose of time is to enable you to learn how to use time constructively. It is thus a teaching device, and a means to an end. Time will cease when it is no longer useful in facilitating learning" (A Course in Miracles, p. 85, Foundation for Inner Peace). What You Think of Me Is None of My Business, By Terry Cole-Whittaker, became a NY Best Seller in 1979. The AA community alerted me to a Church of Religious Science in La Jolla, California. I joined Reverend Terry's church as it rapidly became the fastest growing church in America. These were exciting times, and everyone could feel the energy. I volunteered to help with the guest services and greeting committee and quickly became the coordinator. We occupied the California Theater to accommodate the rapidly growing church. Television crews filmed to produce nationally over the airwaves. My recovery community friends would frequently inform me that I was captured on National TV. It was only a few seconds showing me greeting parishioners as they entered our church services. It was fun and exciting, and glory to God. Service was my purpose. "T-1.I.16. Miracles are teaching devices for demonstrating it is as blessed to give as to receive. They simultaneously increase the strength of the giver and supply strength to the receiver" (A Course in Miracles, p. 86, Foundation for Inner Peace). Reverend Terry's enthusiasm and energy were inspirational. "T-1.I.17. Miracles transcend the body. They are sudden shifts into invisibility, away from the bodily level. That is why they heal. T-1.I.18. A miracle is a service. It is the maximal service you can render to another. It is a way of loving your neighbor as yourself. You recognize your own and your neighbor's worth simultaneously" (A Course in Miracles, p. 85-86, Foundation for Inner Peace).

Meeting Raymond Aaron and Mary Morrissey

"T-1.I.19. Miracles make minds one in God. They depend on cooperation because the Sonship is the sum of all that God created. Miracles therefore reflect the laws of eternity, not of time" (A Course in Miracles, p. 86, Foundation for Inner Peace). Raymond Aaron is my mentor, publisher, and wisdom teacher. I love Raymond and learn so much about the principles of life, wealth, and happiness. I joined his 10-10-10 Program for writing my book, joined his Monthly Mentoring program, and took his Mulberry Hill Gang. He published my first book and taught me about creating no time, spirituality, and creating my economy. Thank you, Raymond, for this opportunity to join in this collaborative Postulate Like A Pro book. "T-1.I.20. Miracles reawaken the awareness that the spirit, not the body, is the altar of truth. This is the recognition that leads to the healing power of the miracle" (A Course in Miracles, p. 86, Foundation for Inner Peace). Thanks to Raymond, I am on a first-name basis with Amazon, type "The Authorities Douglas," and my book shows up on Amazon's URL book title search.

"T-1.I.21. Miracles are natural signs of forgiveness. Through miracles you accept God's forgiveness by extending it to others" (A Course in Miracles, p. 86, Foundation for Inner Peace). Mary Morrissey was an inspiration and catalyst for my pursuit of a doctorate in clinical psychology. If it weren't for her Dream Builder Live events, I would not have enrolled at Walden University for a Ph.D. in Clinical Psychology. At this time of this writing, I am in my last elective class and on the verge of starting my dissertation process. Currently, as a Brave Thinking Master class member, I am grateful to say that my dream is becoming more and more realized as my paradigms rise to offer an opportunity to get in touch with my opposites. Next, I will discuss those opposites in shadow work.

Shadow Work with Ken Wilber

"T-1.I.22. Miracles are associated with fear only because of the belief that darkness can hide. You believe that what your physical eyes cannot see does not exist. This leads to a denial of spiritual sight. T-1.I.23. Miracles rearrange perception and place all levels in true perspective. This is healing because sickness comes from confusing the levels" (A Course in Miracles, p. 86, Foundation for Inner Peace). According to Deepak Chopra, the integral theory was developed by Ken Wilber, the philosopher of our time and the Einstein of consciousness. I have been an enthusiast of Ken's work on Integral Theory for several years, taken many of his courses, and was granted permission to teach his works by Corey DeVos of Integral Life during an online presentation he hosted with Beena Sharma and Susan Cook Greuter. On Earth Day 2020, shortly after the Worldwide Pandemic of the century occurred, Corey permitted me to teach Integral Theory to community college students. He offered to provide content and materials. Thank you. Although I presented the concept to the community college leadership, the lockdown response to COVID-19 has deferred further developments on the initiative. The Integral approach includes shadow work, which was one of Carl Jung's various interests in psychoanalysis. The polarities that Beena Sharma teaches aligns with the opposites and integration of the dichotomies.

Soul Over Mind

"T-1.I.24. Miracles enable you to heal the sick and raise the dead because you made sickness and death yourself and can therefore abolish both. You are a miracle, capable of creating in the likeness of your Creator. Everything else is your nightmare and does not exist. Only the creations of light are real" (A Course in Miracles, p. 86, Foundation for Inner Peace). Meeting Dr. Master Sha through Peak Performance with Adam Markel was an enlightening experience in 2016. A shift in consciousness took a dramatic leap forward, and postulates occur naturally. I did not refer to the postulates experience until I met Raymond Aaron, and how I met Raymond was through Adam Markel's organization. The healing experiences and demonstrations were authentic, and I subsequently enrolled in the research process for my healing wellness. My postulate, I believe, brought me to that probability event. I had hoped to experience soul communication and received results. My postulate brought me back to Raymond Aaron to continue deepening my understanding of spirituality. Raymond introduced me to Jack Canfield, and I joined Jack's coaching club. Marianna Williamson initiated a 365 lesson review of the ACIM Volume II (A Course In Miracles workbook) for students one year ago. I took the 365 daily lessons that concluded a year later over this weekend, coincidentally on Raymond Aaron's Thriving Post LockDown weekend conference—March 27 and 28, 2021. Co-Authorities to my book: Marci Shimoff and Bob Proctor were featured guest speakers in Raymond's event. Are these coincidences of a celestial speed up of postulates? I believe so. What do you think? com

I would go into my relationship experiences; however, for now, that story will be reserved for another time. Thank you for your interest.

Ho'oponono

I'm sorry

Please forgive me

I love you

Thank you

(Hawaiian prayer)

References

1. DoubleBlessed.com
2. Foundation for Inner Peace. A Course in Miracles.

For more information on Douglas Mercer, go to
www.DoubleBlessed.com

MY MOMENT

Selma Pereira

My life has been a continuous journey filled with many different obstacles that has it rewards as well as setbacks. Since a young age I have always had strong determination to succeed in life and be a help to others. These were the values instilled in me at a very young age by my parents. I saw how they worked hard on a daily basis to provide and nurture a family of 9 children. It was not easy for them but they managed through the difficulties and I promise myself that I would do better for them. Now living my life with my family, I still find myself searching for something better. How can I improve my life and my financial situation so that myself and my family can further succeed?

I knew there was a way and that soon enough I will figure it out, but let me tell you at times you do feel discouraged and hopeless as the end of the struggle and tribulations are not there. Fast forward to more recent times, I find myself again working hard to provide for my family, still thinking that there will be a better way to live and work less. It was a Friday evening, working at my part-time job. I was just about to finish; my last task is cleaning up the washrooms when a lady walks in. I continue to clean up the washroom and then she approaches me as she is about to leave. She starts up a conversation with me and then later asks if I would be interested in attending a meeting on Saturday that could change my life. She told me I could bring my husband a long and that there were no commitments but just to come by and listen. I told her I would let my husband know and that we would see her tomorrow.

Once she left I could not stop thinking of the fact that maybe this was the change I was looking for all along. Come Saturday, my husband and I attended the meeting, and later we discovered this was what we have been searching for. This is when we had made the agreement to join WFG/WSB (World System Builder) family and work to help me, my family members, friends and people around me to understand how money works and become financially independent.

I did embrace the WSB Financially Literacy Campaign. I am a WSB Campaigner and we through Financial Literacy Campaign are here to help families like you and I to reach our dream goal of become our own Money Manager. You will learn how to Save Money and how to Make Money. Let's make money works for you instead of you being working for money.

Isn't it powerful?

This was my postulate moment I had been looking for. I am finally living my better life; a life I have been dreaming about it. This positive moment in my life has helped me as a motivation to help others in achieving their dreams of becoming financially free. I want others to see the power of thought and perseverance. We are capable to do whatever we put our minds into it and we need only to BELIEVE and putting into ACTION. Action speaks louder than words. Life is energy and energy is always moving. Teamwork is powerful. There is power in agreement.

My Coach Raymond Aaron gave me his definition of Money and it blew my mind. "Money is Agreement backed by confidence" by Raymond Aaron. I invite you all to join me for the Financial Literacy Campaign with WSB Campaigners and we together will create a better world.

To connect with Selma Pereira by email spereira538@gmail.com or by phone at 647-284-7517

HOW I MANIFESTED MY HOUSE!

Margaret E Prescod

Tasked with finding a house with the profit from the sale of my home after paying off the mortgage and shared ownership was a serious challenge! House prices in London were prohibitive. Initially limited to a houseboat, a holiday home with six-to-nine-month occupation only, a retirement purchase (returning to the seller at my death) or a leasehold house, flat or converted shed or garage! I had started the search as soon as I had the mortgage balance 'shared ownership' and my valuation quote and fees. I skipped the £40,000.00 upgrade costs and opted for an auction sale instead. I accepted a pre-auction price £50,000.00 over what I was expecting at the auction.

I had intensified my search during the twenty-eight days before completion with packing and a large skip load of decluttering! I booked eight weeks of Air B&B accommodation for immediately after the handover of keys. This was most unsatisfactory even after two attempts! I finally found a room to rent with self-catering and could resume my house hunting from a more comfortable base! Eight weeks has passed my storage for £100 was over and now upgraded to four times that amount. I was hemorrhaging money on rent in London, storage of my household effects and country wide house hunting train tickets, hotels and taxis!

I was very hasty when I found this one auction property and it looked better than others I had seen. The property was elevated off the ground. Inside there was evidence of recent painting with no smell of signs of damp! I rushed to my first auction and put a ten percent deposit on it. I had secured a solicitor some days before. I then booked a surveyor who told me the truth! The smell of paint had completely masked the extensive damp. There were also serious structural repairs the council had landed on the owner. This was going to be very expensive to make good! I decided to withdraw from the sale and lose my deposit fees and all! I widened my search areas and resumed house hunting.

Having looked at about two hundred houses, conducted ten more surveys, stayed and searched in Midlands and North of England I was no closer to buying my second house fourteen months after the sale of my property! The Chinese New Year had passed. I set up my wealth corner and made a mood board for the house I wanted, furnished it and put a fun price I wanted to pay for it. A strange word started popping into my head "Johnson, Johnson"! I did not know anyone by that name and it was not in any auction catalogues I had. 'Johnson' the only other reference I had was 'Johnson' American slang for a male sexual organ but I never use the word!

I had a number of properties left to visit including a two-bedroom semi-detached property in an isolated area in the town I was looking at, it was a beautiful house.

I finally visited the property. It was in a beautiful location and the picture was of the back of the house so it looks as if they had a lovely front lawn.

The property was in very good condition, very spacious, very light, no signs of damp and the seller really wanted to move to another country so it was a quick sale. The only disadvantage was that a public path at the side and the back of the property rendering a garden more like an open park and what I thought was a beautiful front garden turned out to be a public path where all people walking could see into your property there was zero privacy. Although it was not overlooked it was very exposed from the sides and the back.

Next day I received a phone call from one of the estate agents. I have visited several of their properties and even had a survey done. A property had come in. No photos yet. A viewing could be arranged while I was in the area. It was similar to one I had seen. The property would be coming up for auction in a few days.

I got a lift to the property.

On arriving at the semi-detached house, I loved the outside front garden with a welcoming hanging floral bush. There was a backyard and two small sheds in the rear yard slanting away from the back wall.

I recorded a video as I walked around the house room by room. I sent a copy of the video to one of my offspring to get their opinion of what I've seen and yes it looks pretty good. I was handed a picture of the property then. A two-page document I just slipped it into the side of my bag and accepted a lift back to town. I walked back to my hotel.

The other properties on my list had access challenges! One house the owner was out at the appointed time! The other house, the estate agent was unable to get hold of the owner for a viewing! Back in my room in London I remembered the folded photos of the property. I took it out and there in small writing was the name of the road Johnson! The asking price was £5,000 above the price I wanted to pay for it!

I wrote my name on top of the photo and thanked God for my new house! I rang my surveyor and left a message on his contact number! He was on holiday but would be able to visit the property on the afternoon of the auction and give me a verbal report in time for the evening auction. The full report would follow by email.

New roof, no damp, excellent condition. I could offer £5,000 or even £10,000 over the starting price! I booked my ticket and hotel!

On the day of the auction, I traveled down early and registered at the auctioneers with a £1 deposit so I could pay my deposit by bank transfer!

I went to the auction where there were two other bidders. The opening bid was by a representative of the auction house. A second bidder was just someone at the back I didn't see any of the faces and then they stopped and I thought well you OK I made a bid and my bid was accepted £3,000 less than the fun price I wrote on my mood board!

I was shaking a bit as I filled out the forms! This was now my house!

What was amazing was the fact that I had heard about this property and had not seen a picture! All the things that I've written down were there on 'Johnson' Road! Wow!!!

To connect with Margaret E Prescod by email at mamakhosinolizwe@gmail.com

PROJECT HEAVEN ON EARTH

Martin Rutte

Twenty years ago, I was getting ready to do a keynote speech at a conference on spirituality in the workplace.

I was sitting quietly by myself in a room off the main conference room when a thought popped into my mind, "If every business in the world is spiritual, is that what you want?" I thought, "No, that's not what I want. Because business has such power in the world, if we can transform business, we can transform the world."

And then a new thought popped into my mind, "Oh, you mean Heaven on Earth."

"You can't say that," I thought. "You can't talk about Heaven on Earth. Heaven on Earth isn't possible. People will think you're some kind of nut, some kind of zealot."

But the more I thought about it, the more intrigued I became.

Why can't we talk about Heaven on Earth? Why can't we talk about the kind of life, and work, and family, and nation, and world....that our Soul deeply longs for? We can certainly talk about all the hells on earth—pandemics, environmental degradation, wars, refugees, terrorism, and so on.

In that moment I knew that the next major phase of my life was an exploration of what it would take to actually have Heaven on Earth be made real in our world. It was Heaven on Earth as more than a good idea. It was Heaven on Earth as something concrete, something you can see and feel.

I had no idea where to begin so I started simply asking people, "What's heaven on Earth for you?"

I'd begun an inquiry—an ongoing question. The more times I asked the question the deeper and wider Heaven on Earth appeared. Think of a business person in the inquiry, "How do I make my business more successful?" The person keeps asking the question no matter what he or she comes up with. It's in asking the ongoing question that the 'magic' happens.

And so I began my inquiry into what heaven on earth is and how to make it show up in the world.

I had a very clear intention and I kept it front-and-center. I continue holding it to this day. When you hold a clear intention, miracles begin showing up. Events and people come into your life that you could never, ever have imagined.

One of the other things about holding an intention is that you have to be willing for whatever shows up to be perfect and use that to forward your intention. I remember a meeting, early in my career, when a very powerful business executive told me my idea would never work. I looked at him, said, "Thank you," and kept on going.

I knew and I know that I am moving Heaven on Earth forward. I call it Project Heaven on Earth. 'Project' as the noun, and project as the 'verb.'

After interviewing hundreds and hundreds of people, I synthesized the results into The 3 Heaven on Earth Questions:

1. Recall a time when you experienced Heaven on Earth. What was happening?

2. Imagine you have a magic wand and with it you can create Heaven on Earth. What is Heaven on Earth for you?

3. What simple, easy, concrete step(s) will you take in the next 24 hours to make Heaven on Earth real?

Please take a few moments and answer the 3 Questions for yourself.

And since that day, many years ago, a continuous stream of miracles has emerged from people answering these questions:

- A woman in Hawaii has embedded her definition of Heaven on Earth at the bottom of each e-mail she sends out.

- A police officer in Texas has written a 16-page brochure: *Heaven on Earth for Law Enforcement.*

- A real estate agent has enrolled each of the agents in her office to have $100 deducted off the commission check they get for the sale of every home. That money has created a fund 'A Home for Everyone.' Each year agencies and individuals in the community apply for funds to create 'A Home for Everyone.'

- A newspaper in Dehradun, India, *The Dehradun Street*, has launched a campaign called DEHRADUN: A HEAVEN ON EARTH CITY! The slogan appears on the masthead of the paper along with a column inside the paper on how to create Heaven on Earth. (The Dehradun Street on Facebook).

- A man from Gabon, Africa has launched a Facebook page called: AFRICA: A Heaven on Earth Continent!

- A teacher in Portugal has launched a Heaven on Earth website in Portuguese. It's aimed at the two hundred and seventy million Portuguese speakers in the world: tinyurl.com/ProjetoCeuNaTerra.

To see more projects, go to: www.ProjectHeavenOnEarth.com, where you can also sign up for a free 7-day Heaven on Earth course.

Create your own Heaven on Earth project, hold the intention to make it real, and play your unique part in making Heaven on Earth real in our world.

Heaven on Earth: The New Story of What it Means to be a Human and What It Means to be Humanity.

I HAVE BEEN TO THE PEARLY GATES AND BACK

Lijuan H. Stahl

Truly! It was in a beautiful summer day of 2019. Just to give you a bit more perspective, I was with a bus load of tourists on a 7 days PEI (Prince Edward Island) tour, which consists of visiting to most of the maritime cities in Eastern Canada, starting from Toronto, meandering our way up north with stops at Thousand Islands, Ottawa, Montreal, Quebec, Covered Bridge, Fredericton, St. John, Hopewell Rocks, New Brunswick, Charlottetown, Peggy's Cove and Halifax.

On day 2, the tour bus pulled into a rustic Pioneer Village, where we got to relive the Canadian history of the 1820s through 1920s. The buildings were nicely preserved from that period, the hosts and hostesses of the village dressed in that era's clothing, attending to the houses, the gardens adjacent to the houses, the household live stocks, a mill by the river, at the edge of the village, and of course guiding us visitors, and providing us with hearty turkey pie dinners just like the good old days.

Walking along the unpaved dusty country road, I came upon a two-story house with a nice arch gate leading to the front door and a beautiful front yard with flourishing plants and flowers. All of a sudden, I sensed the clouds above parted ways, sunshine poured in, the sky became that much brighter, and the flowers in that front yard became that much more vivid and inviting. Almost subconsciously, I handed my phone to the nice village guide and asked if she would be so kind as to take a photo for me, "I want to remember being in this place," I said to her, "It felt so special to me!"

"Sure!" she said delightfully, quickly took a photo of me standing by the white arch gate and then promptly handed my phone back, "This house used to belong to the Pearly family……" she went on and on, but I didn't hear a thing after her first sentence. Stunned, I told myself, "I have been to the Pearly Gate, again!"

Story One: The Big River

Simultaneously, a dreadful, frightening, yet heartwarming memories flooded in. I closed my eyes and saw a 6 or 7 years old little girl, bright, happy, naughty, adventurous seeking…. She was running back and forth on a shaky bamboo "bridge" barely a foot or two above a raging big river, giggling, while her friends were watching on the riverbank. Allow me to tell you about that man-made canal in Southern China. It was originating from a huge water reservoir, the canal was about 30 feet wide, 8 to 10 feet deep, it ran a few hundred miles long in spring and summer time, with some side canals feeding off it. The farmers along its web of routes would draw the water from the side canals to irrigate their corps. Because it is man-made, in order to reinforce the canal, its bottom and the two banks were built with concrete. Therefore, the water flow from the reservoir into the canal was much more powerful than that of a natural river due to the restriction of the narrow and deep construction of the canal. The water raged downstream so rapid, with the current so strong, even adults could barely swim upstream for a few feet, fearfully, we call it "the big river."

"Stay away from the big river!" our parents always warned us, because each year, the river would claim a few kids' lives. Unless we swam in the areas that had steps built in the banks where we could reach and pull ourselves up, it was very difficult to pull ourselves out of the concrete banks without anything to hold on to. To make it even more dangerous, there were dams along the way, that sub-divide the water into the side canals for farmland irrigation. Should a kid got trapped under the dam, it would be almost impossible to get out alive.

There were concrete bridges in some major cross ways to allow traffic and pedestrian crossing. But in some small communities along the canal, people simply tied up a few bamboos, secured them to both end of the canal and built some flimsy temporary "bridges" for the convenience of not having to walk or bike to the major crossroad to use the real bridges.

That dreadful afternoon after school, we decided to go run back and forth across the big river. It was thrilling to us kids! Until suddenly, running halfway through the shaky bamboo "bridge", my head was spinning like I was sinking into the center of the earth! Everything went dark, sparkles flew in my mind's eyes. I was terrified! I wanted to scream but could not make a sound! After like an eternity, I fearfully opened my eyes and immediately saw the raging water flew by under my feet, like a freight train beneath me! My head went spinning out of control again, I was falling, I was going to die.... But somehow, I managed to get myself across to the other side of the river and clasped on the riverbank. Heart pudding out of my chest, feet trembling... I kept the secrete from my mom and dad and everyone else that I have been to the Pearly Gate and back.

Story Two: Climbing Hua Shan

As I went through high school and college, my sense of adventure only grew stronger. I was on a quest to hike all of the major famous mountains (shan) in China: Huang Shan, Lu Shan, Er-mei Shan, Tai Shan, Jingang Shan, Hua Shan, etc. A year after I graduated from a Teachers' University and got a job as a high school teacher, I eagerly waited for my summer vacation, which my friends and I promptly went on a hiking trip to Hua Shan, one of the most sacred Daoism holy mountains, known for its out of reach rugged beauty and treacherous climb. Hundreds of years ago, the Daoist monks sought to get far far away from the mundane life and hide way in the deep mountains to meditate.

Watch out! Here we came! In the summit night, we went to bed early; and then the high mountain inn owner woke us up at midnight, and had a minivan drove us up to the trail head. "Good luck, hikers!" the driver said, "Be careful, follow the trail up, you should be able to summit at dawn, and enjoy a beautiful sunrise!" With that, he drove back down the mountain; and we started our self-guided hike up the mountain. At some point, we reached a section of the trail that was a bit more defined and wider, moonlight shined through the pine trees' branches, I turned around, facing my friends and was walking backward up the mountain; and we were chatting away. Something, I had no idea what, stopped me cold, I turned around and to my astonishment, I saw a huge sinkhole steps away from my feet, as I was in front of them, none of my friends even saw it. Had I moved a few more steps, I would no doubt fall into the bottomless sinkhole! "Careful, careful!" my friends reached out to me, and pulled me to safety. We carefully climbed around the huge sinkhole; and continued our hike to the summit, where we enjoyed a spectacular sunrise in the freezing cold atop the mountain. Later on, we learned, it was the summer mountain flood a few days prior that washed out that huge sinkhole that no one knew about. We were not forewarned, but something stopped me at the gate....

Story Three: Tour Du Mont Blanc

Years later, I found a group of friends who enjoyed hiking as much as I did in San Diego. Two to three times a week during weekdays after work, or on a Saturday or Sunday, we would meet up to hike for a few hours, sometimes into the dark nights depending on the trails we chose. We enjoyed the rugged southern California wildness, its divers amazing wildlife, the vegetation varieties and beautiful wildflowers.

One year, I signed up for a 10 days' "Tour Du Mont Blanc" to trek the mountains in France, Italy and Switzerland. There were fourteen hikers from the US, Canada, Germany, UK, Portugal on the tour, and our wonderful guide was a Swiss mountaineer, our assistant guide was a handsome young man from the beautiful mountains of Colorado, US. We were strangers when we first met at the designated hotel for our initial briefing of the tour. The very next morning, the aerial mountain tramway took us up to the famous ski resort in Chamonix, France, and almost immediately we encountered patches of glaciers in the sunny and warm summer day. Along the trail, we became friends and experienced breath-taking vistas, encountered some abandoned farmhouses, witnessed landslide due to the loss of glacier or trees that used to "glue" the mountain side together; and enjoyed the warm hospitality of the tucked away European mountain refugees.

"Wait, I need everyone's attention!" our Swiss mountaineering guide yelled, having stopped us in front of a huge patch of glacier that covered the treacherous mountain, which we must trek across, since there were no other alternative trails on this steep mountain. The guide asked us to unbuckle our backpacks' waist belts, and explained that should we fall, we must let go of our backpack and DO NOT let the backpack drag us straight down the mountain! From where we stood, it seemed bottomless and steep. "Keep your distance", the guide instructed, "we can only go across one by one, and minimize our disturbance to the glacier." Four or five hikers carefully reached the other side and were waiting for the rest of us. It was my turn. I surveyed the terrain and realized there were two sets of shallow foot tracks on the glacier, about 15 or 20 feet apart. The higher track seemed to have sustained a bit more foot traffic, so I chose it. Step by step, aided by my hiking pokes, I carefully got halfway across the glacier, suddenly I slipped, fell on my bottom, and started to slide down the mountain! Faster and faster! "Arrest yourself!" "Arrest yourself, Lijuan!!!" My guide and fellow hikers screamed at me! I tried to stick my hiking poles in the glacier, but it couldn't cut in. Then I felt a bump, and I felt down to the lower trail. I tried again to strike my hiking poles into the glacier, this time it punched through! It stopped me from falling. I closed my eyes to catch my breath, in my mind's eyes, I saw the sky so vastly blue, the clouds so softly fluffy, the warmth flooded my body and my soul as I pulled myself up, trembly and like in a daze, I finished the second half of my trek across the ageless glacier as though I was walking towards the Pearly Gate.

Our beloved Louise Hey, the late publisher, author and American motivational speaker once said, the universe loves me and supports me. I am a true believer of that, and I might add, the universe granted me a few glimpses of the elusive Pearly Gate, so that I can truly appreciate how precious life is and how beautiful our world is.

I am so grateful to have this great opportunity to share my sacredly guarded precious memories with you, thanks to Mr. Raymond Aaron and his wonderful team, so that you may Postulate like a Pro!

Please connect with Lijuan Stahl by email at lijuan88882002@gmail.com

REVEALING THE POWER OF POSTULATES

Charles Tchoreret

Unknown to most people, our mind power is the strongest and most useful powers we possess. This power, together with our imagination, can create success or failure, happiness or unhappiness, opportunities or obstacles. This depends on each individual's mindset. ... Mind power is composed of your attention, your mental images and your thoughts.

This power is mainly fueled by our thoughts, and when focus is added to the thoughts the "extraordinary" happens and very situation that is cause by your thoughts becomes your reality—positively or negatively.

Something that I have learned is that I have the power to determine the way my life goes, in a concise and intentional manner. I insist on the word intentional because any other posture would mean that life happens to me by chance. **Nothing happens by chance, or rather, everything is a consequence of a law: spiritual, mental or material.** The thoughts that pass through our mind are responsible for almost everything that happens in our life.

Millions of people know the daily ill effect of fear, anxiety and negative thoughts in their life; in the same way they know about the beneficial power emanating from a positive, courageous and confident attitude towards life; Yet, few take advantage of the power available to them and apply it to shape the direction they want their life to go. As a result, they exclude themselves from being the actors of their existence by sidelining themselves from applying what can be a source of great happiness for them. How is this possible you may ask? Well! Most people keep deep into their heart, the erroneous feeling that it is a uphill task to attract joy a happiness and success.

Through the next lines, my intention is to bring reader of this amazing book to open their eyes and raise their awareness on this unparallel power within: the MIND.

I wish you all after that awareness, to become authentic artists of your life and through the power of the mind, feel invigorated and confident to fashion the life of your choice, free of fear and anxiety.

Once you experience what your mind can do for you, you will stop dwelling over what could have been or what should have been. You will no longer agonize over lost opportunities or mistakes you have made or others have made. You will no longer spend your present in the past regretting and wondering why "bad luck" is your daily portion.

Life is so beautiful and precious that it's sad to waste it away either in regretting the past or aimlessly dreaming about the future and as a result drowning into the deep sea of sameness, where most people are buried.

Your mind gives you the **power to postulate** on whatever you want to see happening in your life, but also what you don't want to see in it, through what is known as **counter postulate**.

This is not some magical tricks. It is simple coming to the realization that The Universe—God—in you is much more powerful than the physical realm. That godly power is always available to you, however, trapped in the turmoil of life, human being in their majority have lost touch with The Higher Power Within.

Dear readers, may the eternal knowledge of the Universe be your portion as you familiarize yourself with them in this book. May they help you achieve a life of happiness, wealth and success.

My Experience with Postulates

From a very young age, I realized that I could think of something and it would happen. At the time, I thought that it was mere coincidence and I had no clue what to postulate was all about.

I started paying more attention to what was happening in my life more closely when I decided, 12 years ago, to connect to the spiritual realm and the power of God in me. That's the time I understood the spiritual meaning of *Romans 8:28*—"*And we know that in all things God works for the good of those who love him, who have been called according to his purpose.*"

Fast forward, things became even clearer when I registered and attended the strange and wonderful *Mulberry Hill Gang* conference in November 2018. In that event, I learn about the power of the spiritual realm vs the physical realm and how one can, intentionally give pre-eminence to the spiritual realm and awaken the power of God within. This power has always been in me, but it was patiently waiting to be acknowledged and to be positioned in the forefront.

God worked on me in an amazing way—typical God! After coming to the realization of His supreme power, some situations that happened to me a few years back started making sense.

Back in the 80s, I was studying ALS—Applied Language Studies—in London, UK. In the final year of my studies, I had to write a memoir. Unfortunately for me, I did not know how to use a typewriter so I had to, urgently, find someone willing to help me.

That same year in Christmas, I traveled back home to Gabon for two weeks. Two days after my arrival, I called my friend and I told her about my predicament. She generously invited me and accepted to type the memoir for me; so, I flew to her next-door city, thirty minutes away by plane. That was my first time in that place and I literally fell in love with the city. So, I told my friend that I wouldn't mind living and working there after graduation.

Two days later, she completed the memoir she even printed extra copies for me. Talk about having a heart of service!

I graduated in 1984 and flew back home immediately in June. A week after my return, I started applying for a job. I got three offers: Air France, UPS and Tenneco Oil. I decided to accept Tenneco Oil's offer. There I was working in The Oil and Gas Industry. This experience lasted twenty-five glorious years.

Six months after I joined the company, my boss call me in his office to inform me that I was transferred to Port-Gentil, the city where I went three years earlier to get my memoir typed. I postulated about living and working in that city… and it happened.

I had many more postulates that came true since. Some life changing and others very basic; like going somewhere and postulate for a parking space, and it's right there. Among the significant ones, I can say that meeting my wife Carole was, without a doubt my biggest postulate ever. Everything was packaged and received as requested from the Universe. Simply mind boggling.

Happiness Seeker Today and Always

Like all human beings, I always wanted to enjoy a peaceful life. I did not just want to live. I want to live happy. Everything that I do is motivated by that objective. I know that I'm the sole responsible for my happiness and it is up to me to use all the tools I have—material and primarily spiritual—to materialize it. I have to learn to fight the battle between the flesh and the spirit of God in me and ensure that the latter prevails. I know that the Universe—God, is the source of all knowledge already invested in me, all I need to do on a daily basis, is to train and strengthen this mighty power and use it to make changes in my life, and in the world.

Conclusion

I am well aware that the mind power plays an important role in creative visualization and the law of attraction.

If I plant seeds, water them, and give them fertilizers, they will grow into healthy and strong plants. I know that my thoughts are like seeds. They have a natural tendency to grow, get powerful, and manifest in my life, whenever I feed them with my attention and allow them to grow.

My attention, interest and enthusiasm are what make them powerful. If I show lack of interest in a certain thought, it will not gain strength and would not be powerful.

- My thoughts affect my subconscious mind, which in turn, influences my actions in accordance with these thoughts.

- My thoughts might also pass to other minds, and affect other people. Therefore, I have to be careful of the thoughts I entertain.

- At the Mulberry Hill Gang conference, in November 2018, I realized that by sharing and focusing on my dreams and goals, I actually attracted into my life people who accepted to back me up in my *"Africa—A Heaven On Earth Continent"* project.

This is how the universe works, out of the blue it can activate a dramatic change in your life that you will never be able to explain accurately in the physical realm. This is known as a quantum leap.

This might seem strange and unbelievable. You don't have to accept these words, but if you analyze the kind of thoughts you think, and the kind of life you are living, you will discover interesting things. There is a correlation between your thoughts and your life condition.

We all are a manifestation of the Universal mind. The power of our mind is part of the creative power of the Universe, which means that our thoughts work together with it.

The power of the Universe is accessible to everyone. All you have to do is sublimate your spirit of conservation and transform it into an instinct for self-fulfillment, to call on your slumbering creative forces and to activate the inner genius.

Finally, The Universe listens to your vibrations. It responds to the signals you put out. So, if you are putting out feelings of sadness, you will continue to be sad because the Universe responds like for like. Likewise, if you are feeling happy, you will feel more happiness as it is returned to you with abundance.

The parable of the talents in the Bible is a good example of such return of abundance. Three servants received respectively five, three and one talent from their master. All, were asked to use their talents to the best of their ability.

The first and the second servants used their talents to significantly increase the value of the property they were granted. The third one, however, buried his talent and did not enjoy the gains of his predecessor. When called on to account for his behavior, he claims that fear prevented him from embracing his talent. The master reprimanded the third servant for being lazy, and casts him out.

Just like those servants, we are responsible for conducting our life as our mind leads us. At the end of the day, our results will speak for us. Not because we would have accomplished selfish goals, but rather how we contributed, with our talents, to the bettering of people around us and the community we live in.

For more information on Charles Tchoreret, please visit his website at www.charlestchoreret.com or email Charles directly at info@charlestchoreret.com.

NEW VENUE OPPORTUNITIES COME TO THOSE WHO ASK

Eldon Wingay

My name is Eldon Wingay, RMT. I am a Registered Massage Therapist who helps people with Pain, Injury Rehab Mobility, Posture & Attaining Top Performance. I used to work at a karate gym several years ago which also had a Wellness Clinic integrated in their space.

It was located about ten minutes from my home & was on a cross side street off a major Toronto intersection. I used to treat many of the students & the public there for pain, repetitive stress injuries, postural imbalances & lack of flexibility-mobility. One day, the owner decided to move as he had found a better nearby location on the main intersection street of Toronto.

Unfortunately, there wasn't space for a Wellness Clinic there & it was also located on the second floor. Thus ended my time at the first location & I was left out of the second location.

I had been working at that time at another clinic which was about forty-five minutes away & had found employment even farther away across town at another clinic which took about an hour & half to get to. The travel time was lengthy since I was using the public transit system. A couple of years later, I was tired of working at the long-distance clinic for several reasons other than the distance & was looking for a new venue to work.

One day while walking in the neighborhood coming from the bank, I ran into one of the karate teachers I had treated at the old first karate school Wellness Clinic. He was just off to have lunch. I learned that that the karate school owner had just moved a second time & had found a better location on the ground floor level a couple of doors down & was creating a Wellness Clinic in his school. I contacted him & made an appointment to see the karate school owner & started working at his Wellness Clinic.

End result: better ground floor location, closer to home travel time savings & a better financial arrangement!

Please connect with Eldon Wingay at ewingay2@yahoo.ca

www.ingramcontent.com/pod-product-compliance
Lightning Source LLC
Chambersburg PA
CBHW072151090426
42740CB00012B/2219